A Voice in the Wilderness

A Pastor's Journal
of Ground Zero

the Journal of
Camille Ogle Yorkey
October 11 - December 25, 2001

Published by Judgment Ring Books, a wholly owned subsidiary of Expert Systems Programs and Consulting, Inc.

A Voice in the Wilderness — A Pastor's Journal of Ground Zero

From the journal of Reverend Camille Ogle Yorkey,

ISBN 0-9679119-7-4   First Printed Edition
Printed in the United States of America

Cover art by Jack Duckworth

All over-cost proceeds from the sale of this edition are being donated by the publisher to Reverend Yorkey's Hope in the Wilderness ministry.

I dedicate this book to a member of my first congregation at St. Paul in Goldsboro, North Carolina, now an octogenarian radiating vitality in every facet of her life. She edited my ordination papers and over the years has become a longtime, faithful friend as well as editor.

I dedicate this book to

Doris Ward

ACKNOWLEDGMENTS

No worthwhile project is ever completed in a vacuum and this book is no exception. I never meant to write a book. It just flowed directly from my heart out of my fingers. That is exactly where it would have ended if it had not been for the tireless efforts of Jack Duckworth, my Webmaster and the CEO of my publishing company, and Doris Ward, my impeccable editor. Jack, Doris, and I are in ministry together. Without them the 8,000 readers would not have been able to look through my eyes into the life of New York City after September 11, 2001.

For years people have been telling me to write a book, however I never would have done it without the support of the many dear friends who paid my expenses while I did ministry in New York and prayed diligently for my health, and my emotional and spiritual well being. I would never have continued writing the journal without their precious affirmations and encouragement. For them, I am so grateful. In fact, for all the members of my former churches and those with whom I am in relationship I am grateful, because without them in my life there would be no story to tell.

To Sister Grace, the Reverend Lyndon Harris, and the faithful staff of St. Paul's Chapel, New York, I am so very grateful for their ministry and for giving me the opportunity to serve.

To those of who have helped along the way, Maren Symonds, Diane Parker, and Katie Kross, I am thankful and will be eternally grateful.

To those left behind to mourn and to work after the collapse of the World Trade Center towers, I hope I have been faithful in my perception and retelling of their stories. I take full responsibility for any inaccuracies in my observations, memory, or writings. I am so very blessed that our paths have crossed and I am a changed person because of them. I thank those who have shared their hearts and lives with me and for responding so generously to my ministry.

To those who died in the most tragic event in America's history to date, I give thanks for their spiritual presence and for the legacy they leave for us to carry on. From that loss may we learn how to live in a world more focused on peace and unity, and molded by love.

A VOICE IN THE WILDERNESS

Foreword

In the spring of 2000 I got word that a close friend from my late teens and earliest twenties had been stricken with lymphatic cancer. In a story too long to tell here, we had first met in Paris in the summer of 1964, only weeks after we both had graduated from different high schools in Northern Virginia.

The people we know best are the ones we grow to know in that short period of innocence that exists just after childhood, before the trials of adulthood can get a grip on us.

My close and dear friend is Camille O. Yorkcy, one of the most remarkable women of our time. She was a gem in the rough when I first got to know her in the summers of 1964 through 1967 and a fine cut and polished gem when I next saw her in the late fall of 2000.

A diamond starts out as carbon and takes its final form only after being subjected to immense heat, pressure and stress. Camille is such a human gem.

As a writer, I find it exceedingly difficult to not tell you of the Camille I know and love. As a realist, I am aware that Camille is very special and different to everyone who is blessed enough to know her—to talk to her even if for only a few minutes.

I could tell you of the great times and experiences we shared in Paris but that would tell you nothing of the spirit of Camille Ogle

A VOICE IN THE WILDERNESS

Yorkey. Others could tell you of the experiences they have shared with Camille over the intervening thirty-eight years, but those would also tell you nothing of her indomitable spirit. The most revealing words are her own.

What follows are thirty-eight entries from Camille's journal. They chronicle the highs and lows of her tenderhearted sharing of the grief of the friends and relatives of the victims and of the heroic workers at Ground Zero. They chronicle not only the pain and suffering of their losses but also the joy of their small and grand victories.

As Camille so aptly points out, time and time again, each of the heroic individuals feels that he or she is contributing almost nothing to the unbelievably complex and difficult task and yet, collectively, they are accomplishing what is likely the most grand, most difficult, and most heart-wrenching undertaking of this new century.

As you read her journal, you will be moved to tears, as Camille frequently is, for you will see Ground Zero through her empathetic eyes and heart. Sometimes you'll even be moved to laughter which will please her.

You will discover that the opportunity to see any of the world through the eyes of the Reverend Camille O. Yorkey, even if only for a few moments, is truly a blessing.

Jack Duckworth

A VOICE IN THE WILDERNESS

E-Mail
The Calling - Raleigh, N.C.
October 11, 2001

Dear Friends,

God's timing is everything. Last Monday my doctor said, no more blood work is needed for eight weeks and I don't have to see her again for four months (both had been every four to six weeks). My lymphoma is dormant. It is wonderful news and I feel great! So, I had immediately gone to the conference office and said "I'm ready to work."

Tuesday, I was called by UMCOR to come to New York City to do crisis counseling with families of the WTC attack. UMCOR will provide a room (with a bath down the hall, hmmmm) and I will be raising my own support or just volunteering. However, it is a gift to me to be able to reach out in this way and I drive up next Tuesday, October 16th for a two-week initial time period.

Who would have known that two years ago, after the flood, my position as Director of Pastoral Care for Disaster Ministries would have given me the perfect experience to do this; and even the fact that my husband was killed in his thirties will help me relate to these families. It reinforces our understanding that each and every experience we have changes our lives forever. Even our moments of grief are precious and transforming.

Thank you for your prayers and love, both past and future. We are all in this together and I carry you with me in my heart. Knowing you has changed me!

Many blessings to you and those you love,

Camille

E-Mail
The Preparations - Raleigh, N.C.
October 12, 2001

Friends,

I have been overwhelmed with your many offers of support and questions concerning how else you might help. I won't know all of the answers until I get to New York. However, today (with the help of a couple of friends) I started an outreach organization, (more paperwork to follow), opened a checking account, got a treasurer with an address, and a Board of Directors, got my 'cable functioning computer' set up for dial up correspondence, and asked for a room with a phone line, if possible. So, in response to many questions about how you can give financial help, if you or your group or church want to support this outreaching financially, you may go to the donation page to make a donation.

This will not be an overnight "fix," because as we all are experiencing, grief is a process. . . a long process. Once again, thank you.

Many blessings,

Camille

A Pastor's Journal
Entry One - NYC - Ground Zero
October 17, 2001

I'm in my hotel room. I've been in only one room worse than this in my life. It was the summer of 1964. I was supposed to be staying in Masion de Nederlands, a dorm at the University of Paris. Instead, I was on the Rive Gauche (Left Bank) in the Latin Quarter with an artist, for a few weeks.

My room here in New York is probably eight feet by ten feet. The one in Paris was smaller. This room has a pedestal sink with a mirror near the door; that one only had a miniature sink (like on airplanes) in the far left corner. For light, this room has one floor lamp; that one only had a bulb in the ceiling. This one has a place to hang about 20 hangers; that one had floor space for a book bag and backpack. Both had only one twin bed.

Thank goodness, in this one, I am alone. There are no pictures and there is no window to open. The air conditioning is not working. The bath is way down the hall. But I have a roof over my head and am protected from the elements, and that is more than our soldiers in Afghanistan have, and more than many of the civilians there ever have. All of the displaced families from Ground Zero would be grateful. Those who lost innocent family members in the WTC attack would give up all physical possessions just to have their loved ones one more time. So, shut up, Camille, and be thankful you brought your own pillow.

When I returned to the hotel at 10:15 p.m. on the day of my arrival, a uniformed man stood at the door asking if he could help me. I replied, "I live here."

He said, "Yes, ma'am. Please show me your key."

Fifteen steps into the hotel, I was greeted at the elevator by a young uniformed woman who said, "May I help you?"

"1218," I replied.

"Please show me your key."

Before today, no one in a hotel had ever checked to see that I was a guest and had a key. The world has changed. I'm afraid the world has changed forever. But then, we've all known that since September 11, 2001.

Never in a million years would I have thought ministry for me would mean standing on a corner in Manhattan, by myself, in the dark, saying to each passerby, "Hi, how are you doing tonight?" The doors to the church sanctuary were wide open behind me, so I wasn't afraid... well, not much. I spoke to hundreds during the 5:30 to 7:30 p.m. rush hour! It was truly a microcosm of the world—people of every size, shape, nationality, lifestyle, and socioeconomic level.

The young associate pastor had assured me it was ministry in New York City just to make eye contact and smile, and any kind of response I got would just be icing on the cake. And if I actually got anyone to come into the church or to talk... well, stars in my crown, you know.

I kept recalling my daily morning prayers: "Just let your light shine through me, God, let me be your instrument, increase my territory. [Prayer of Jabez] Let your influence through me be increased. Keep me from evil so that I cause no pain." But, God, standing on the street corner in NYC in the dark, alone, smiling at people??? Perhaps I had expected a nice, clean, air-conditioned office with easy chairs and a couch and a new box of tissues, where I could really show off my pastoral care skills. But I know down to the marrow in my bones that God has called me here to serve, however that might be.

Most passers-by looked at me as if they thought they might be on candid camera. All but a couple smiled back at me. Those that didn't gave me a look like "It is just none of your damn business how I am tonight." A large majority gave me a second look—a surprised look—and said "good" or "fine" or "ok." But then some were talking on the phone or listening to CDs or radios, and I just didn't bother them. There were several memorable people. . .

A large, handsome African-American male, dressed to the nines, walked on a few paces after I spoke. He nodded, then came back and said, "You aren't from New York, are you?" "No." I stuck out my hand and said, "I'm Camille Yorkey, and I'm a pastor from North Carolina up to help with families and friends of the terrorist attack." "How long have you been here?" he asked. "Just a few hours," was my response. With a broad, friendly smile, he said, "Welcome, Camille. Thank you for coming, and I hope your stay in New York is fabulous." He walked on. But the lump in my throat remained through the next fifteen hi-how-are-you-doings. He was so kind.

A limo pulled up, then double-parked. A tall, thin, beautiful blond (she looked just like Anne Heche) got out of the backseat. Her hairdo was adorable and I told her so while the limo waited. She came up to me. I asked her if she wanted to come inside the church to chat, and she said, "No, thank you, but do you mind if I just go up to the front of the church and sing a little. I think it's ok. I have done it before." "Sure," I said. She smiled in gratitude. She sang for five or ten minutes while the limo waited. She thanked me, got back in the back seat, and left. Well, I sure didn't do any ministry there, I thought. The terrorist attack didn't seem hurt her any. But she had a precious spirit and the voice of an angel.

Three-quarters of the way through my evening on the corner, a Caucasian man in his mid-to-late-thirties came by. He was obviously very drunk, staggering drunk. I started not to speak, and then instantly was reminded of the Igniting Ministries program I have been teaching for the last seven months. "Open Hearts, Open Minds, Open Doors." God's church is open to ALL.

He was dirty, had a week's growth of beard, was wearing tattered clothes, and his nose was running... even into his mouth, perhaps because of cocaine... but then how would I know? He would have been quite handsome if not for his condition. When I spoke to him—"Hi, how are you doing?"—he stopped, staggered around a little bit and tried with much difficulty to focus his eyes on me.

A wave of panic passed through me. It took only an instant, but I heard all of the warnings and fear-filled messages of a lifetime in one heartbeat. He slurred out the words, "Not too bad, how about you?" After replying that I was fine, I asked if he wanted to go into the church for quiet time or prayer. He held up his palms toward my face and said, "No way, not like this," and he tried to wink. "Ok, then. I hope you have a good night."

He walked off as I breathed a deep sigh of relief. Just as I was exhaling, he turned around and staggered back... my heart fell. He smiled a huge smile, crooked and quite ugly in his condition. And he said, "Thank you, thank you very much." I cried, and just nodded my head. He cried and walked off. I really haven't done much ministry for those affected by the terrorist attack, yet "whenever you do it unto the least of these, you do it unto me."

At 7:30 pm, I went to a seminar given by two psychologists on dealing with life after disaster. There, I was able to help a young woman understand the stages of grief so she can allow herself to process through them. I listened as a foreign-born man (Oh, my ignorance at not knowing the people in God's world!) at least six-foot-five tear up as he told me that he was afraid to ride the subway and it was hurting his ability to get to work on time. Another woman, overwhelmed with fear, was dealing with the issue that no customers were coming into her furniture store and when they did, they couldn't concentrate and just wandered around, not buying anything. I listened, but felt helpless. I had no words of wisdom. I just held her hand.

At nine p.m., I got back on the subway and rode home alone, wondering if I had been any good to anyone. Climbing four flights of stairs out of the subway, I opened my eyes only to see the Chrysler Building burning all of its lights. It appeared so strong and proud... a majestic sight. Life goes on.

I had dinner at 9:30, listening to a couple in the booth behind me—he old enough to be her father—discuss how they could not be together this weekend because his wife was coming into town. She was sorrowful, but the discussion went on about his daughter and her four children who live in... Chapel Hill. I instantly felt embarrassed. Why? Because I was drinking a glass of wine with my eggplant Parmesan ($23—I feel guilty about the price, but know I must eat healthfully and I needed this food since I'd had no lunch), and he might know I am clergy? Or because they might know through osmosis I am clergy and would condemn them? Or because I was eavesdropping, since our heads were only eight inches apart, separated only by six inches of bright green naugahide? Maybe in times of crisis and fear, we acknowledge how very fragile and fleeting this life can be. We know that love comes in many forms. That discussion is for another time.

Note: Must remember to talk about the huge bronze statue of a fireman kneeling, with his back bent and head in hands, with flowers all around it on the sidewalk near Ground Zero.

Also must talk of the large woman I've seen three times at the elevator.　She has dark black dyed hair, mismatched flower-print, check, and striped oversized Salvation Army attire and lives here all the time.　Absolutely starved for conversation.　Maybe she is my ministry.

I must remember how I went to the wrong level in the subway and waited for number four or five as my paper told me to, but only number six came by.　I didn't get on.　Not the first number-six train or the second one or the third one.　Everyone looked at me so strangely—I just pretended I was waiting for someone.　I finally got on the fourth, thinking, "What is the worst that can happen?"　Later, the associate pastor told me I had gone below the ground level two floors to the express platform; number six was the fastest.　Hmmm, good job, Camille, by default.

I must remember to talk about my feelings seeing the skyline with out the twin towers for the first time as I was entering the Lincoln Tunnel.

Must remember to talk about the firehouse with the pictures of the firefighters who lost their lives in ministry to others, posted on the board outside, and the flowers and cards pasted on and around.

It was so strange tonight to see fresh flowers on each table in that restaurant when there was no toilet paper or paper towels in the bathroom. It seemed strange also to walk out of the restaurant and see a man rummaging through the garbage left on the street and a young couple close by kissing and hugging. Back to reality: "Ma'am, do you have the key to your room?"

I'm hot, but must go to bed. Maybe tomorrow I will do some real ministry.

I thank all of those who helped make it possible for me to come. Thank you, thank you, thank you. I am where God has called me and am where I am supposed to be right now. I am the one who is blessed.

A Pastor's Journal
Entry Two - NYC - Ground Zero
October 18, 2001

I absolutely can't write as much as yesterday. It took too much time and I was so wound up and exhausted that I couldn't sleep. On my first trip to the women's restroom (way down the hall) this morning, I was overwhelmed with the smell of pot. I was too hot during the night to be able to sleep well. The room was so depressing and had such bad feng shui (I'm really going to spend two weeks here???) that I decided to call the desk, tell them I would pay the difference myself if I could just have a bathroom. They said that my room was $90 a night; one with a bath was $140 a night, but I didn't have to think about that because they didn't have any available. My heart fell.

"However," the cheery voice said, "I have just had someone leave from a room where only two rooms have to share a bath on a small adjoining hall and it is the same price as yours. Do you—"

"I'LL TAKE IT!"

Repacking and unpacking... a small price to pay. Now, there is room beside the bed for my suitcase to be used as a night stand and since there is NO air conditioner in the window, I have some daylight, because it faces the street instead of a brick wall. The window will even raise two inches for ventilation. There are three black and white postcards framed on the wall for decoration: the Empire State Building, the lion in front of New York Public Library, and the lobby of Grand Central Station. This room even has two plug outlets so I can run the computer, charge my phone and keep the only lamp on at the same time. Thank you, God, for my new room! Having the experience of the other one reminds me of how very spoiled I am. Even though I keep a gratitude journal daily, there are so many things that I take for granted, that I never even think to be grateful for.

The woman with the black dyed hair was in the hallway as I waited for the elevator on the twelfth floor. I now realize that she is always there in the hall, just hoping to have some human contact with anyone. She talks fast. I now know it is because she has to get everything said before the elevator arrives. Good for her they are slow! In just one afternoon, we talked about ballroom dancing, Leonard Bernstein, the good old days, terrorism, and England, her home country. I actually felt a little guilty leaving her standing there. What was that look on her face, as she saw my suitcases and just said, "Bye"?

I spent several hours in the UMCOR offices upstairs. Beautiful locations on the 17th floor, a small balcony (A thermostat to control the temperature! I'm impressed.), several laptops humming all the time, and cell phones ringing constantly, each with their distinctive songs so that we can tell whose is ringing. Ann stays very busy, screening possible volunteers, checking references, getting their District Superintendent's blessing, filling out the appropriate forms, and giving directions. I realized I was extremely proud that she is from the North Carolina Annual Conference UMC and was chosen because of the marvelous job she did running the disaster office during the Hurricane Floyd disaster. She is the wife of a pastor and they are a blessed team, a credit to the whole Methodist denomination. Brian (a full-time UMCOR volunteer, I think), Ann, Rick, and I discussed how to attract people so that they would know what we have to offer. He mentioned that this was the project of the New York Conference (Oh yes, of course, but then we all feel like this terrorist attack was done directly to us, don't we? The disaster does belong to New York as far as UMCOR is concerned.) and that they have plans to offer an ongoing job-fair type place and they already have the spaces in the city. WOW! That is a biggie. I said I was sure that informal pastoral counseling (he used the words "spiritual counseling") could be offered at the same time, like part of the process. "Sounds good!" He then said that would start in maybe two or three months.

So I asked Ann if she would design a nametag for me to wear on the street that could be seen and read on the street. "...No, not 'Reverend.' Just plain Camille Yorkey, Pastoral Counselor in large bold print, with the small UMCOR insignia red flame and cross, and the UMCOR phone number so that my credentials could be checked out."

"Two heads are better than one," my grandmother used to say, "even if one is a sheep's head." Well, I was definitely the sheep's head, but it took three of us to get it perfect. Now it is a template for other volunteer pastors.

Since there were really no plans for me, I asked to go to the scene of the disaster. I bought a $20 metro card, using my credit card in a subway machine (many new experiences).

It is "not proper" to make eye contact on the subway. However, I noticed as people looked at my name tag, they would make eye contact... and almost smile. Is this ministry? As I rode the Lexington line to the Brooklyn Bridge, I thought about something Ann had said. It seems that she must do so much screening, because some pastors don't understand that ministry in this situation is non-judgmental (novel idea!), that it is for the purpose of healing and transforming pain into new life and not changing lifestyles or cultural differences or even religious preferences. It seemed sad to me that she had to tell pastors that. She and Rick discussed "a loose cannon"—a pastor who would not follow directions, would go anywhere on his own and attempt to judge and evangelize, perhaps using the disaster as fuel and proof of his mission. It makes me sad and not proud to be associated with someone who would manipulate the weakened to further his own religious agenda.

Walking up the steps out of the subway, I was aware of the blisters on my feet and the sore muscles of my short, stubby legs, when right at that very moment, I saw on the steps ahead of me a young, obviously professional woman in her beautiful, long, leather coat. Her light auburn hair fell in meticulous ringlets below her shoulders and her designer pocketbook holding documents as well as personal items hung from her back, draped around her shoulders. Then, on her very long and slim legs, under a long kidskin skirt, were leg braces. I could only see the part attached to her boot-like shoes. I had time to notice all of this because I was behind her and she had a metal cane attached to each arm and was very slowly negotiating each step. We were two floors below ground!!! My gratitude journal is becoming more superficial all of the time!

At Ground Zero, as I walked west from the subway, the first thing I noticed were the many police barricades. Other than that, there was nothing distinctive about the place. I simply said, "God, let me be your instrument."

In front of a seriously guarded City Hall, I walked over to four young policewomen, wearing bulletproof vests, uniformed with large handguns and billy clubs. Now, I don't usually go up to police officers—perhaps it is the fear that I might be doing something wrong or because I am such a pacifist that being even that close to guns scares me. But I went over, introduced myself showed my badge and said that I just wanted to offer time to chat together, informal groups to debrief, bitch, support.

We built relationships; before I left them we had exchanged names and phone numbers and I had learned that two had actually been in the building during the collapse. One said she had been overcome with smoke and debris and given up. She had always known she would eventually give her life in the line of duty, but she hadn't expected it to be this soon. When all at once, she heard someone screaming for help. She said on "autopilot," she moved toward the voice and they both made it out alive. She said she owes her life to the one screaming for help. My dear friends, that will preach!

I asked the two whether they had nightmares. With widened eyes they looked at me for an instant like, "How did you know?" And then immediately looked away with tears in their eyes... after all, they are police officers and not afraid of anything. I wasn't so brave—the lump in my throat became salty tears making their way down my face. How was I ever going to be of help to anyone if I couldn't even control my own tears?

They thought it would be a good idea for me to meet the officer in charge of community affairs and said she wasn't too far away. One actually took me to her. She was extremely open to the idea of my working with them, and as I wrote her phone number on the back of a card, small flakes of debris landed on its white surface. I was so overcome that it was difficult to keep writing and not to just look around at the sky and be overwhelmed at the task.

She said that during mealtimes, the firefighters and the police all ate at St. Paul's and that I could do a lot of good if I could get inside with them and listen to them and simply be with them. Wonderful idea, but lots of red tape. I think Ann is working on getting me inside. St. Paul's is the church that didn't fall down even though its steeple is blackened from soot. At the point of barricade, there are still people playing violins, flutes, and guitars. However, now their tunes are mainly patriotic. I put dollar bills in each of their cases.

There are still flowers and candles there, but not as many as at St. Vincent's Hospital in Greenwich Village. Having dinner with a friend in the Village, we walked to "The Wall," where all of the pictures are displayed. The sadness is so overwhelming I can't begin to explain. On the ground in front are plastic fire hats, children's cards, hundreds of candles expressing the large Catholic population, flowers that have been dead now for weeks, but still are piled up, as if removing them would mean we might begin to forget. Nearly every picture has a type of simple biography attached. Pictures of loved ones holding their infants, playing with children, laughing at parties, dressed in wedding gowns... Then I saw a photo of a young woman with a huge smile. It was a close-up of her from an attached picture of her with three girlfriends. They were toasting each other. Her birthday was the same day and same year as my daughter's. I couldn't read any more.

A Pastor's Journal
Entry Three - NYC - Ground Zero
October 19, 2001

Typing all of this is taking more time than I want it to, and I'm in my room more than I want to be. Early today, I had to refill a prescription, so stopped at a market on the street and bought flowers for my room. I always have cut flowers at home, either from my yard or from the grocery store. So my hotel room feels pretty much like home now. Even the noises of horns honking and sirens blaring, all night, becomes rather comforting after a while. The street noise is especially apparent with the window open (no screen?). It keeps me from feeling so alone as I sit or sleep in my room.

The UMCOR office is working on the possibility of my going into St Paul's for meals with the workers. Evidently, it is very political and will take a lot of coordination with the Episcopalians even if it is possible.

While I was riding one of the packed subway trains today, a neatly dressed man got on and got everyone's attention by saying, "Let me have your attention, my name is Moses (actually he looked like Moses) and I haven't had anything to eat today. If you could just please spare a little change for some food. God bless you."

There I sat right next to him wearing my big name tag with the cross and bright red flame. New Yorkers don't want anyone to give money to panhandlers, and I think it is actually illegal for them to solicit on the trains. I knew I have so much more than he does... whatever his motive!!!

I always stop my car and give people $5 or $10 in Raleigh, when they are on the street corner begging. I'm driving a Lincoln, look much too well-fed, have a beautiful roof over my head... and why would I not? If nothing else I know my self-respect is higher, no matter what their motive or how much money they get begging on the street or how they use it. I do worry about the pattern though. Give a man a fish and he eats for one day; teach him to fish and he eats for the rest of his life. Do I give it to make me feel better about me? It is just a quick fix that really does no long-term good.

When no one gave the man on the subway anything, he said, "I promise I will use it for food." Perhaps it was my imagination, but I was afraid those on the train were looking to see what I would do. I knew not to just blatantly give him money. It is important to respect those who ride the trains every day and are not just visitors. So, after a minute or two, I very discreetly reached into my pack attached around my waist and got out a dollar. My plan was to give it to him as I got off at my stop further down the route. However, he got off at the next stop . . . probably not wanting to be caught. My dollar was still wadded in my hand. Hmmm, he had on a red, expensive-looking nylon windbreaker. I followed him with my eyes as the train pulled on. Obviously, he wasn't meant to have my measly one dollar.

Fear is evidently the overriding feeling that permeates most of the residents of NYC.

My shoes have rubber soles. A pastor asked me to go into the sanctuary where a woman was sitting alone to see if she needed to talk. As gently as I could, walking up behind her, I said, "Excuse me," and she jumped in panic. I thought she might have a heart attack.

She said, "I've been afraid of everything lately."

I told her that irritability, anger, generalized fear, and acute fearfulness are all a part of dealing with the threat of terrorism and the trauma of the terrorist attack. She shared that no one she knew, or was in any way connected to, had died in the WTC attack, and she felt very guilty about feeling so depressed. She told me she couldn't sleep. I admitted that I couldn't either, and that her reactions were entirely normal. She cried and said she felt so guilty for being old and still being alive (survivor guilt) when all of those young people had died needlessly. (I didn't cry this time.) She also said she was sorry that she had lived long enough to see something like this happen. We talked about God's timing, not our timing.

She feels so helpless. Don't we all? Just talking made her somehow feel better. She left and thanked me profusely. But, God, what did I do? What did I really do? Thank you for just letting me radiate your light, love, and acceptance. Fear can be so debilitating; it truly causes emotional and physical pain. I am convinced fear is a huge roadblock to healthy spirituality.

After all, fear is the opposite of faith. I heard last Sunday in a skit in church (what this has to do with anything I don't know): "If you are afraid to love, you are afraid to live, and if you are afraid to live, you are three-quarters dead already." I refuse to be fearful. Cautious, yes, but fearful? Never.

It is a good thing that I am not debilitated by fear. After talking to another police officer at the precinct who gave me directions—"Take subway train four local, get off at City Hall, walk three blocks, and get on bus M22 about fifteen minutes to our corner"—I walked to the subway to get on train number four, when everyone started hurrying up the steps saying, "Go back, go back! There has been an explosion on track number four!" I came back to my room to watch the TV news. It said nothing about an explosion. It did say that four, five, and six were all closed for police activity . . . whatever that means! So I didn't get to the precinct today. But I will soon.

I don't think I'll watch any more news today. I do believe in the wisdom of the saying, "God, grant me the serenity to accept the things I cannot change, change the things I can, and the wisdom to know the difference."

Today I talked to two young women in different places, and at different times. Both of them wanted to retell their entire story of where they were, what they were doing at the time of the attack, and what the rest of their day was like. One has a sister in Greensboro, North Carolina. Out of the clear blue sky she said, "I think I'm going to move. Do you know anything about North Carolina?"

"Well, yes," I said. "I graduated from college at Greensboro College in Greensboro. It is a very nice place to live."

She was on the subway on her way to college and was under the WTC when it happened. Oh my gosh, I had never even thought about the subways! They felt the jolt and the quaking, but she said she was not as afraid then as she is now. Her fear and uncertainty of the future has made her unable to maintain her daily routines. She said, "I am afraid to live here. Most of the anthrax scares have been here." She works in a pharmacy and said there has not been a run on Cipro, but she is constantly afraid that there will be.

Both women talked about all of the cell phones and other communications being out because the antenna towers were on top of the WTC. The other woman was a young Jewish girl who said that, since she worked on Wall Street, her mother had been frantic after the attack, not hearing from her. It took her five hours to walk across the bridge to the Bronx after she walked up to the northern part of Manhattan.

It is very apparent the benefits of any ministry here will be achieved only one person at a time. Hmmm, isn't that something we talked about in Igniting Ministry? It is frustrating, but much like the story of the starfish. There was a man standing on the beach, picking up starfish, and tossing them one by one back into the ocean so that they wouldn't die. Someone came along and, looking at the starfish in the man's hand, said, "You know, there are so many out here, you can't save them all. What you are doing really doesn't make a difference." The man tossed the starfish far out beyond the surf, saying, "It really makes a difference to that one!"

A Pastor's Journal
Entry Four - NYC - Ground Zero
October 20, 2001

I spent several wonderful hours with a newsman. He is exactly the age of my children (too bad!). As I was sitting at my computer at seven p.m., a sudden panic hit me and I heard a voice, not another's voice, but my voice. *What am I doing? It's a weekend and I'm in New York.* My spirit has always been fed by theater and music. The voice said, *"Get up."* It's seven p.m. and I don't even know what's playing, or where. *"Get up anyway."*

At 7:10, I was downstairs waiting to ask for a New York Theater booklet (hidden, by the way, in stacks under a table somewhere... probably most of the people in this hotel never have the opportunity to go to the theater). Looking at it two seconds, I decided on *Mamma Mia.* Why? I don't have a clue. I went out to catch a cab, hoping I could get a seat at the theater. Of course, there were no cabs; everyone was going to the theater (or somewhere). I started walking. It was dark. Could I make it by curtain time? I hurried, stopping several times to ask directions. It was about 20 city blocks.

At 7:50, I was at a window waiting for tickets. The woman in front of me heard how much the tickets would be and turned around to ask me if she should pay that much. I asked where she was from.

"California. I'm just here to prove that the terrorists can't make us afraid."

"Of course," I said, "pay the money. You can't take it with you; money is only good for how it brings happiness and joy to you and to others."

"Right you are." She told the man that she would take two seats.

I was next. He said, "I'm sorry—sold out." Oh, if only I hadn't told her to pay the money!

He said, "Sorry. It looks like tonight everyone is trying to show his or her support. Hardly anyone has been attending the theater since September 11." Yes, but I am so disappointed... (What will be will be).

He told me to go start a line for cancellations out front; ask the bellman. When I got out there, there were 20 people in the line. Oh my gosh, I must have cut in line. Now how would I ever get in? Slowly, the people in front gave up. The couple ahead of me said they didn't know what to do, so I pulled out my recently acquired trusty theater booklet and off they went to *Music Man*. The bell chimed for the show to start. Now, there were one man alone and a couple in front of me. The man got a ticket. But when the couple in front of me heard that there was only one seat left they began to argue loudly (and New-Yorkishly) over who wanted to see it more. He ended up saying quite obnoxiously "You take the damn ticket, I didn't want to see the old play anyway!"

At that, the man in the booth discreetly pointed to me, motioned for me to give him my credit card. He told them there were no more seats available. Yehhhhhh!

I told him it was worth coming to his booth twice, just to get the last seat.

He said, "I thought you did it just to see me."

"I did," I replied.

"Do you like my new haircut? I got it just for you," he said.

"Yes, do you like my new sweater? I wore it just for you."

"I like it," he said, and, "Enjoy the play... you got the last seat in the house." Praise God!

I sat next to the young man waiting in line in front of the arguing couple. We bonded immediately over our good fortune. However, it wasn't two minutes before I knew he was meant to be sitting by me and I was meant to be sitting by him.

He is a newsman, and it was his mother's birthday. She had died in April (on my birthday, but I didn't tell him). He came to honor her by attending the theater because they always went to plays together. She loved to laugh and clap and dance and basically enjoy life. They were best friends. I knew immediately that we were meant to be there together that night. My children and I are best friends and I take them to NY to plays. They good-naturedly tolerate my singing and dancing (we tease about me dancing on tables... I never really do it... just always threaten to do it). Within thirty seconds, I had told the young newsman I would be his mom for the night.

We loved the energy of *Mamma Mia*. The house was full, in support of the arts in spite of the tragedy. It is important to go on with life in the midst of tragedy.

I couldn't help thinking, while I was sitting there clapping, laughing and at times even singing with the cast, that there were thousands of families not too far away whose hearts were still breaking. When my husband, Randy, died 21 years ago, the only one I had ever known who died was my aunt in Texas; and I didn't attend her funeral. One huge shock to me was how very angry I was that others' lives went on in normal fashion. Couldn't they tell that my life had fallen apart and nothing could ever be the same? But then, I came to understand that we do walk through the valley of the shadow of death and God is with us. We do not stay in that valley forever, when God is with us.

During intermission, we discovered that he had gone to NC State University for undergraduate studies. I forgave him. I had gone to Duke for my Masters of Divinity. He worked in Raleigh politics; I now live in Raleigh. He had gone to George

Washington in DC for his masters; I had graduated from Mount Vernon high school in Alexandria, not far from there. His family lived in San Francisco, California; I was born there. Hey, maybe we were twins separated at birth? Dream on, Camille. As soon as the play was over and he said, "Do you want to go somewhere afterward for something and talk?"

I immediately said "Yes." If he hadn't asked me, I would have asked him.

Of course, our conversation was difficult for him. It was important for him to retell every detail of the last few weeks, days, and hours of his mother's life. The death, destruction and sadness of the terrorist had brought all of his feelings to the surface.

Many people are experiencing renewed sadness related to past losses, while not understanding why they have these feelings. I was reminded once again of the words of the speaker at Convocation last Monday. He explained the healing power of telling and retelling the story until it is no longer painful.

I received an e-mail from Rod Grindell in Maryland. He had surfed onto my web page. I don't know him, but he is a firefighter and EMT. This is what he had to say:

> Something in your on-line journal jumped out at me: "How was I ever going to be of help to anyone if I couldn't even control my own tears?" As a firefighter and EMT, I think the answer is: You

did help them by showing and letting them know that it is OK to "let their emotions out" and yes, even to cry.

Fire & EMS people are accustomed to suppressing their emotions, because they have critical jobs to do and emotions get in the way of getting their jobs done. The public expects and needs strong, confident emergency-services personnel. Who would follow the directions of a crying cop or trust the medical judgment of a whimpering EMT? Besides, you can't see well when you are crying! (:>)

Even though they can sometimes rise to the level of superhuman to get the job done (witness 9/11/2001), these folks are human too. That emotion often stays bottled up inside, causing long-term, debilitating psychological damage. Many of these folks will be going through the classic "Survivor Guilt" (why did I make it, when my buddies did not) and "Monday Morning Quarterback" (if only I had done...) syndromes. Remind those who are discouraged and want to quit that this is not a one-time test (even the WTC was attacked once before). Unfortunately the need for their services continues day after day, in big ways and small, and that the best way to honor those who died is to carry on.

The emergency services departments have Critical Incident Stress Debriefing (CISD) teams, but I am sure they are overwhelmed by the number of personnel involved and the magnitude of the incident. You mentioned that "ministry in this situation is non judgmental." Well, often the emergency services folks won't "open up" in the CISD sessions, because they are surrounded by peers and fear that they may be considered wimps or might be taunted later about their emotional statements.

As a counselor, you know these people will open up only to someone they trust and who is non-judgmental. As a "person of the cloth," you are uniquely qualified for this job.

We used to have a joke (which of course is no longer funny) about the entrance test for the fire service: "There is a fire... do you: A) Run away like most sensible people or B) Run into the burning building?"

Tell them they passed the test and that their brothers and sisters in the Fire Service across the country salute them for their bravery and sacrifice.

His words hit the mark. I'm sure there is a scripture that can be quoted about the importance of being there for one another and allowing each other to grieve and shed real tears, but I can't quote it.

Healing requires true openness, but true openness runs face to face with a huge trust issue. Some pastors who have come to me for counseling have shared the fact that they don't trust other clergy, or anyone in the system, enough to be really REAL (sounds like The Velveteen Rabbit). It is sad, but I understand it and experience it as well.

I shared my thoughts of the firefighter's e-mail with my theater-companion newsman; for over two hours after the show, over ice cream and shakes, he was open and real. The pain that had been uncovered by the special significance of his mother's birthday and the sadness in the aftermath of the terrorist attack was exposed and hopefully eased. If we perceive God's call on our lives... on our every moment of our lives (even in the theater!), we can serve as an instrument of God's grace and light. And I pray for that daily... so why wouldn't I listen?

My newsman friend told me of the sadness he feels for the families that his TV news station had put on the air those first few days, those who were desperately looking for loved ones who were missing. I know that now they are somewhere, close by, possibly all alone. The hype is over, and they have been left with the certainty of death and the accompanying emptiness. It is no longer a news story. How do I get to them? It really is a challenge that UMCOR is facing at this moment. How do we get to them to let them know what we

have to offer? Most of them don't even know what they need.
They are just hurting and suffering alone. I can't fix it, but I
can be with them while they hurt. It isn't everything, but it is
something.

When Randy died, I got a brief note from Margie Day, the
wife of our Associate Pastor at Washington Street UMC in
Alexandria, Virginia, when I was in high school. Her husband
Bill had just graduated from Divinity School at Duke. Women
didn't go into the ministry back in the early sixties, at least
not any that I knew of. Hmmm, I probably should have gone
then. Anyway, Margie Day sent me the most powerful note I
had ever received. It simply read, "Camille, I cry with you."

A Pastor's Journal
Entry Five - NYC - Ground Zero
October 21, 2001

I must remember to thank my dear friend Jack Duckworth, my webmaster (whatever that is!). We knew each other in the 1960's after high school graduation, when our fathers were both stationed in Paris, France. (Now, there is a book to write!) He and his wife live just south of Washington, DC. By day, Jack works for the government; by night he works on my web pages and his stories. In his heart, he is an author.

We renewed our acquaintance only last summer when everyone thought I might die and had many old friends visit. Jack and Andy (our "third Musketeer" in Paris) were among them. We got together after not seeing each other for 34 years. We all looked exactly the same... NOT! But we did act the same, and the ties that bind, and the laughs, are still there. Jack has written a bunch of short stories and four short novels, part of a series called the Judgment Ring Books, www.judgmentring. com. Two have been published. Jack designed my web page, has been encouraging me to write (actually, he's been a pain in the neck, hounding me not to stop!) and has been inserting, on the web daily, everything I write.

I must not forget to thank Katie Kross, a dear friend and neighbor, who has been editing my keyboard peckings and fixing the spelling errors before sending it on to Jack for insertion.

I must also remember to tell those in my conference (the North Carolina Annual Conference of the United Methodist Church) how wonderful it is to have their support. Daily, I get encouraging e-mails from clergy and District Superintendents concerning both my ministry here in New York and my journal entries. Here is the e-mail I got from my bishop, Bishop Marion Edwards.

> Camille,
>
> It is good to hear from you and to know that things are going wonderfully well for you healthwise. We give thanks for such a wonderful blessing!
>
> I am most grateful for the new ministry you have begun. My prayers and thoughts are with you as you head to New York to work with those who desperately need your help.
>
> I know that God will bless you and those to whom you minister. Keep in touch!
>
> Marion Edwards

We are truly an interrelated and connected denomination. That fact is nowhere more evident than when we are attending another UMC, in another state, and another conference. Yesterday, I worshiped at John Street United Methodist Church. It is terrible of me to admit, but as a tourist in New

York, I had never actually been to a Sunday morning worship service.

John Street is the matriarch church in Methodism. It is the oldest continuous Methodist congregation in the United States and has been meeting since 1766. In 1768, the first building was constructed on the present site and was named "Wesley Chapel" in honor of (of course) John Wesley.

I didn't remember that New York City was the capital of the United States after the Revolution, but it was. All types of people worshiped at John Street: sailors, clerks, artisans, soldiers, housewives, slaves, mechanics, carpenters, and shopkeepers. (That's brief History 101!) This historic church is right in the heart of lower Manhattan, just a few hundred yards from the World Trade Center. The view as you step out of the door of the church and look to the left is one of rubble, cranes, and darkened facades. It is daunting. Yet, worship continues.

It is far from home, but when I stepped into John Street UMC, I was home, for there was my sign: "Open Hearts, Open Minds, Open Doors. The people of the United Methodist Church." I was so at home it was unbelievable. This congregation lives the truth of that sign in its makeup, in its obvious acceptance and tolerance, as well as in its welcome. It lives that truth more than any other church I have attended lately... or possibly ever, including my own.

I could tell at once the pastor was brilliant. Not necessarily the "tall steeple" type of brilliance, nor a part of the hierarchy-of-the-conference type of brilliance, but the kind of brilliance that makes me smile when I hear that the brilliance originated and graduated from Yale "undergraduate school" in the early fifties.

I had to struggle mentally to keep up with a lot of our conversation, which involved his storytelling and belly-laughing and the two of us sharing such totally "brother and sister" clergy stories. I was truly humbled by the God-given genius this man possesses (but he's not and never will be computerized... he did condescend a couple of years ago to move to an electric typewriter... but that's it!) Here is the Morning Prayer, concerning the World Trade Center disaster, reprinted with permission of the brilliant and inspiring Rev. James (Jim) R. McGraw. It is a beautiful sermon all by itself. Please, be blessed by it, as I was. Oh, how I wish you could hear it from his booming dramatic bass voice!

> O, God, our Creator and our Redeemer, Sovereign of the universe and ruler of nature and nations; Thou, who are the ground of our being, the source of our strength, the wellspring of our hope, and the one and only solid and reliable rock, in whom we place our total trust . . . Hear us now as we turn to thee in prayer.

> We stand this day, O God, on a threshold of a familiar numerical reckoning in the annals of

our faith heritage. Forty days and forty nights the rains fell in the days of Noah; forty days and forty nights Moses communed with thee, atop Mt. Sinai; forty years thy chosen people wandered in the wilderness, on route to the Promised Land; forty days and forty nights Jesus fasted before being confronted with the temptations of the Evil One; and it has now been forty days since our own encounter with Evil at the World Trade Center.

On this day we feel a kinship with those other moments from our faith tradition. In the flooded subway stations deep beneath the toppled towers, we are reminded that the torrents, which descended upon Noah, came down to wash away violence, corruption and evil. In the images, which will never be erased from our minds and our memories, smoke and flame descending upon the pinnacle of the south tower, and panic in the plaza among the people below, we are reminded of the fire and smoke which enveloped the top of Mount Sinai, and of the people of Israel trembling and quaking at the foot of the mountain.

The forty-year journey through the wilderness wasteland, where deprivation gave rise to doubt, and what began as a stride toward freedom, detoured in the direction of grumbling and regret, remind us of the hardships we have felt and the emotions we have experienced during our own forty days in the wilderness named THE FROZEN ZONE: displacement from home still a painful reality for many in our neighborhood; phone service still absent from so many homes; electricity only recently restored; mobility restricted to the annoyance of many, the home incarceration of some, and the financial disaster of countless merchants.

With these and with Jesus, we too are tempted at the end of forty days to ask, How long, O Lord, how long? Will the life we have known and all too often have taken for granted or have taken as a privilege deserved, rather than earned, will it ever return? How long until normalcy reigns and the present restrictions imposed upon us be lifted? And yet, on this the fortieth day, we find ourselves still mired in fear and trembling.

With the images of terror from above still raw upon our wounded and grieving hearts, we are now confronted by terror from within. The dread of anthrax infection looms so very much larger than the reality of persons thus far infected, and fear spreads faster and further than the detection of disease.

As the sighting of anthrax moves from Florida to Washington D. C. and to New Jersey and New York, the mathematical equation of terror calculates one dead, one close to death, forty contaminated; equals a whole nation gripped by fear.

In such a setting, O Lord our God, we hear thy Word once again calling up out of the clutches of fear and into the assuring embrace of faith. We hear again Thy Word which echoed from a Bethlehem hillside to an empty tomb: "Do not be afraid, Christ is born and Christ is risen, and death is swallowed up in victory." Do not be afraid.

Towers may topple and lives may be consumed, but the ultimate consummation is that death is swallowed up in victory. Do not be afraid. The evil or the deranged may tamper with the mail, and others suffering from terrorist dementia may load up baggage lockers with bombs in a suitcase, but death is swallowed up in victory. Christ has died for one and all and we have nothing to fear. O, God, may we live in fact by what we know in faith. May we live each day according to the Good News of the gospel rather than the bad news of the moment. May we be victors of promise rather than victim of panic, walking by the light of thy Word rather than plunging into the darkness of the world. . . . Hear us as we pray. AMEN

And to you, journal, AMEN

A Pastor's Journal
Entry Six - NYC - Ground Zero
October 22, 2001

Last night I talked to my mother on my cell phone. She said, "How do you like your suitemate?" (using the term 'suitemate' rather loosely).

"Mother, he lives next door, and I haven't even seen him."

"Him? Your suitemate is a man?"

"Yes, he is a man."

"But, Camille, how do you know he's a man if you haven't seen him?"

"Mother, we do share facilities you know... he leaves the seat up!"

I saw the woman with the dyed black hair yesterday on the street, when I was walking to the subway. I was pleased to see a familiar face. But she acted as a child does going to a birthday party. She was that excited when I spoke to her. Her mind is childlike. I don't think she really remembered me, but she started talking fast just the same. She chattered about how much she liked Dan Rather, about how she lives just around the corner in a terrible mess, and about how nice people used to be in the old days. I made a few brief comments on the great weather and how good it was to see her (I meant it!).

She kept chattering as she walked away toward the hotel. A few days earlier, she would have been one of those people on the streets of New York whom I probably would have avoided. There is good news though; I don't think she is even affected by the terrorist attack on the World Trade Center. She may not even know!

When Bob and I moved to Wilmington, North Carolina, before starting Harbor UMC, I made noises at first about wanting to live in the old, restored section of downtown. He would have no part of it. I thought it was because his heart belongs near the water. But he said that it wouldn't be safe for us, especially with the large population of street people in downtown Wilmington. What he meant was, "They look different, dress different, smell different, and because they are very different from me, I don't want to be around them."

However, times and people do change. About a year later, after he had been working at the pharmacy downtown for a while, he said, "Remember when I didn't want to move downtown because of the street people?"

"Yes, I do remember that."

"Well, now I call them all by name and they call me by name. I'd say on some level, we're friends. If they ever ask me for anything, I give it to them. Sometimes they even try to pay me back. They are nothing to be afraid of, that's for sure." It was powerful to hear him admit that he looked beyond their exterior to see who they were as real human beings.

Too often, we judge just by looks. With the information from the recently mapped genome, which reveals the fact that throughout the world, human makeup is 99.95% exactly the same, why is it that we tend to focus on our differences rather than our similarities? After all, what real difference does color, or race, or religious preference make? We are all human creations of God.

When I was working as a chaplain at the Baptist Hospital in Winston-Salem, I worked in one ward where everyone was in the last stages of life. There, I quickly discovered that it dosn't matter whether the patient is Methodist, or Baptist, or Holiness, Pentecostal, Muslim, Jew, agnostic, or atheist, because their pain, fears, hopes, and needs are all basically the same. It became my job, as an instrument of God, to speak a language that would communicate love, hope, and concern to each of them. Following the events of September 11, perhaps we are all beginning to understand that universal language at least a bit more.

On the street late yesterday afternoon, I saw a cute little woman in her late seventies, or maybe eighties, with pink hair (Hey, I've had a few strange hair colors myself.) Not just a bad dye job, but also a perfect Pepto-Bismol color (it was totally white at the roots), with matching lipstick. She obviously felt beautiful. We all want to be accepted for who we are. We all want to feel beautiful and we want others to speak our language, no matter what form our packaging takes.

A sector of society that is not used to tragedy is now suffering. Many of those who died in the WTC attack were in their thirties and already affluent by average American standards. The standard of living is quite high here in New York City; I believe I remember reading that it is second only to Paris, followed closely by London. However, the pain of such loss observes no economic or social boundaries. The survivors, some of whom are in serious emotional pain, don't look to be in need of anything. For the most part, they are the young, attractive, "yuppie" types, and appear by all physical standards to be healthy. But the real people, the people on the inside, are hurting.

One young man, who survived the attack only because he was on vacation on September 11, is suffering terribly as a result of the events. He has education, money, prestige, good looks, health, and clout, yet his heart is breaking.

He fears he is heading for a serious "meltdown." He worked side by side with many of those who died. He worked with them, day in and day out, from seven a.m. till dark, those high-powered brokers in their cubicles, sticking notes on one another's backs, playing jokes to lighten the tension, tossing paper airplanes, and (what I call) "solving the problems of their world."

He pulls out pictures from his 31st birthday a few months ago, saying, "See these four guys standing with me in this picture? They are all dead. See this man? He was supposed to retire at the end of last month, but stayed on one more month. He was my mentor and now he is dead."—The mentor looked young to me, maybe in his forties—"See this girl and the guy she's with? Both gone. See this guy? His wife found out that same morning that she is pregnant. He's gone, too. See these three crazy guys making faces at the camera? They are all gone, too. All of those people were at my birthday party and now they're all gone."—Yes, I think, it's more than most will ever have to bear in a lifetime.

He continued, "Work for many is almost impossible; reconstruction is monumental. We are working to give all of our profit to the families of our employees who died. So my income is down. People don't know what they are doing now. It's a small thing, but I didn't have any water this morning at 5:30 and had to go to the Y to shower."

As I listen, I experience a fear, a fear that there are, and will continue to be, too many unhealthy responses to this type of pain. There will be too much alcohol and drugs, too much or too little food or sleep, and too much superficial contact just to avoid going home alone. I've been there... anything to dull the pain, even if only temporarily.

There are many stories like his and they need and deserve hours' worth of sharing and listening. It makes me feel unbearably helpless, almost. I know "that which does not kill me makes me stronger, and God will not give me more than I can bear." Easy for me to say. From my viewpoint—looking back upon a life filled with ups and downs, dealing with family death, family on drugs, divorce, disappointment, and disease,

I can see how each trial has made me stronger. It was true for me, but it is impossible to share that 20/20 hindsight with a generation that has had known only triumph and is now experiencing a loss of inconceivable magnitude.

It seems to me that these tragic events are affecting the Gen Xers more than any other group, those born between '64 and '81, who have not had to get in their grade-school halls on their knees, with their hands over their heads for air raid drills. These post-modern Americans never faced Viet Nam, neither as supporters nor anti-war demonstrators. The National Guard has never held them back on campus during race riots. They have never had to face the death of their president. These people have not participated in freedom marches through the streets of Montgomery or Atlanta. They don't know what it is like to be told, "Women don't (understood as can't) do that." They have not had to fight to prove that women are capable. The terrorist attack is truly a bitter pill for this successful and untested generation to swallow.

Several of the young people I have spent time with in the last few days have used the term "surreal." I'm not even sure what that means. But I got their point. It is not the time to preach, "Without a spiritual well within, there is no safety" or "Our only strength is our Christ-like self within, luring us always toward wholeness and wellness and completeness and joy even in the midst of trial and tribulation." No, now is not the time to preach those things, perhaps that time will come. Now is the time to listen, to share the pain, and to hear the cries for help.

For the time being, I made a referral. My concern over this young man's use of the term "meltdown" is huge. UMCOR "crisis counselors" are called listeners for a very good reason.

There is more to tell, but not now, not in this position, at the laptop, with my hands cramped, and my neck and back hurting. I'm tired of writing and have become exhausted from the intensity of every conversation. I would be alone except for the wonderful encouraging e-mails, which I dearly look forward to, even though it might be weeks before I get around to answering each.

At this point, my need to be out among the people is stronger than my need to write. I know I will be surprised today—as I am every day—because I just can't tell by looking at people what is going on with them on the inside. Looks can be so deceiving. All I can do is ask them, "Is there anything I can do to make your life better today?" It doesn't seem like much.

A Pastor's Journal
Entry Seven - NYC - Ground Zero
October 23, 2001

I love my hotel, surprise, surprise. It feels like home, now that I'm on a semi-regular schedule. Brian in the UMCOR office explained to me at lunch today that not only was it the best room price they could get in the whole city for the volunteers, but that the hotel threw in all of the gorgeous top floor for UMCOR offices. As well, it was a huge help to the hotel, because the management was going to have to cut many employees' jobs for lack of tourism after the terrorist attack. The main reason UMCOR chose Habitat Hotel was to show the public, and all of Methodism, that those of us who are here are here for ministry and not sightseeing in one of the most famous cities in the world. I agree wholeheartedly and am proud of UMCOR for its decision. We are blessed when decisions are made with integrity for ethical reasons and with stewardship in mind.

Bob was not and is not a sentimental person. Back in the mid 80's long before we got married I used to get flowers from others. He would say, "If you ever get any from 'anonymous' they would be from me." Well, over the years, he tried to take credit for many such occasions, NOT. However, it is still a standing joke between us. Yesterday, I got a beautiful peace lily plant delivered to my room. Even the florist looked surprised that such a lovely plant was delivered to such a "quaint" and humble setting. There is just room to put it in the corner and not hit it when stepping out of my bed on the way to the sink. I love it. What wonderful life it brings (good oxygen too) to my room. There was no name on the card. Hmmm, it must be from "anonymous." Now, of course it is not from Bob (even though I still wish it were). Still, whoever the sender, the sender is loving, thoughtful, supportive of my ministry here . . . and generous. We are a people who need to be in generous relationship with one another, more now than ever before.

The attack on the WTC came totally without warning. Who will ever forget the terrifying pictures picked up by the TV cameras of those individuals who jumped out of windows, a hundred stories above ground level, as the towers were collapsing? Who will ever be able to erase from memory the unimaginable image of people jumping, holding hands as they began to fall through the air? Perhaps no other visual can express more vividly how much we need each other in times of crisis. We do need each other.

The attack on our nation and the threat of anthrax spreading every day—three now dead, and more hospitalized—offer us a unique opportunity to find intersections with other human beings. This is an opportunity to find intersections in expression and communication, but even more so on a soul level. It is uniquely at the soul level where our actions are truly in generous relationship with one another, for it is within the context of relationship that we are able to sort out our myriad reactions to this horrific event, to explore the meaning of life, and to be able to make valuable connections between not just our actions, but our thoughts as well. What WE do and say and think make a difference in the WHOLE WORLD!

Each one of us is accountable because we are each a facet of the diamond, put together to make the whole jewel of humanity. Thus, we are a people who need to be in generous relationship with one another.

I grieved for years over the loss of my marriage and the loss of that special relationship. Even typing this today I feel a little guilty thinking and writing of my own past grief, all the while knowing the magnitude of the loss found outside of the safety of my hotel room. However, every feeling that we have, each loss that we individually face, and all grief that we experience—all are uniquely ours and cannot be put on a graded scale or compared with others. All have lead us to where we are at the moment, the right place for us.

Take for example the young woman with a blond-gray ponytail, dressed in business casual, from the John Street neighborhood (she is a graduate of Carolina also, by the way—once again, I forgive). She lives only a few hundred yards from the barricade. In our conversation she expressed guilt over her mundane concerns in the wake of such enormous tragedy. She had lost friends, many friends, with the destruction of the towers; she worked in a business in the basement of the WTC and saw those people every day. Yet, when we really got into what was upsetting her at that moment, as we talked, it was the ordinary part of her life that had been disrupted. For example, most of the subway stops near her house are still closed . . . indefinitely; her cat can't go out on the balcony because he is old and the fumes and debris in the air might kill him; the bookstore where she and her husband got coffee every day is boarded up; her husband must walk much further to work because of all the barricades and must go through several security checkpoints even within his own building; the neighborhood grocery store is gone; her Krispy Kreme donut shop may never reopen (she really felt guilty about missing that so much.)

As she talked I noticed her glasses were covered in the debris and ash still permeating the air, to such a degree that I was surprised she could see.

Many of her fundamental assumptions, in fact her entire world view, had been destroyed in a single violent day. Nothing makes sense. She feels a loss of security and well-being. What she was basically telling me was that life, as she had known it, would never be the same. Oh, how very true. Lives as we all have known them will never be the same. No, they never will be the same . . . BUT WE CAN BE BETTER because of it.

There is no one right way to grieve, and it takes as long as it takes. No need to feel any guilt about our own problems or pains in comparison to the unfathomable tragedy in NYC. We are where we are and God loves us right where we are, at every moment. Learning to live in the presence of grief is a long, slow, painful process, one that probably never ends completely. But time and prayer change us, in fact transform us.

Another family has a child that wants to move, because they too, were in the WTC neighborhood and live in a tall building. The child has it in his head that bad things happen to tall buildings. He is afraid and it seems that moving is his only concept of dealing with the fear. That is not just a child's perspective. As adults we sometimes think that moving will take away our fear or our problems. If we just get out of this relationship, the next one will be better. As pastors we pine, "Oh if I had another appointment in which these little old women didn't complain about everything I do, and if I had a better Pastor-Parish Relations committee. Oh if I just had a little more money my ministry would be better. Oh if I just had more clout in the conference, I know I would be happier." None of that is true. Our only true happiness and safety is within.

If I have a glass of water and my finger is in it . . . changes occur only when I take MY finger out of the water. When I take my finger out, every single molecule in the glass moves—it must be a law of physics or some kind of law. It makes the wonderful point that I can control only my own actions (i.e. motives and thoughts) but the consequence of my doing so is that every molecule in the whole universe responds. Love is the answer. Love is the only answer. "God is love."

Of course, many of the children here are afraid. I was with one mother who said her child was afraid at night. The child was sure she had 'terrors' in her room, under her bed, in her closet and they were coming in through the door when she was asleep. "Terrors" of course were terrorists, perceived as monsters. It pains me to see the innocence of our children destroyed by the evil of a few. They now know too much of the painful truth about the world. I can only imagine the 'terrors' that the children in Afghanistan experience in the face of our bombing. The therapist suggested that the child should have a flashlight by the bed and use it like a "ghost buster" (Good idea for all children afraid of the dark!) The therapist said, " 'Terrors' are afraid of the light." That too will preach.

All of the darkness that comes into our world and into our specific lives, in whatever form, can only be understood and transformed when the light of the spirit of God shines on it, in it, and through it. That spirit is closer than a flashlight beside our beds. It shines within, at the very core of our being, and is expressed outwardly in our deeds and words and especially our thoughts, those innermost motives and intentions. Only then can we be free from fear. "The light shines in the darkness and the darkness will not overcome it." 'Terrors' are afraid of the light!

A Pastor's Journal
Entry Eight - NYC - Ground Zero
October 24, 2001

A year ago today, my lymphoma had the upper hand in the war for my life, and the battlefield I chose for my counterattack was a detox treatment center in North Carolina. It was sort of Eastern in nature, but open and accepting of all faiths (thank goodness) and to all expressions of spirituality. It was truly a holy experience. Only two cancer patients at a time can be housed in the center's sparse, sterile environment.

We prayed over everything from the incense to the enema bags. I was consuming wheat grass, a form of laetrile, and was cleansing my body of the toxins thought to be a contributing factor to lymphoma. Anyway, the procedure was well worth a try. Everything we wore had to be cotton or natural fiber, and we couldn't wear anything that had been worn in a public place until it had been washed (in a natural cleansing product, of course). We took off our shoes at the door.

I spent most of the two weeks on huge white cotton-covered pillows scattered over the spotless hardwood floor, feeling sick, sick, sick, and trying my best not to throw up. I listened to tapes from medical intuitives, holistic healers, nutritionists, and ayurvedic specialists. I awoke to the sound of Tibetan bells and the sweet scent of white sage.

Romans 8:28 has always been my favorite text; "All things work together for good for those who believe and are called according to God's purpose." Boy was that scripture ever true, as demonstrated in the grace that I experienced at the treatment center. (Yes, I'm still drinking my Super-food, green algae and taking all of my supplements even up here in NYC.)

The woman who indirectly referred me to the center, through my wonderful Duke counselor, was also a patient at the clinic for two weeks last November, but she died during the summer. We never know who or what is going to change our lives profoundly. Therefore, the importance of being conscious and grateful in every moment cannot be underestimated. For me, having lymphoma and spending two weeks at my treatment center have been precious pivotal points in my own spiritual growth. In relation to this tragedy in NYC, however, my hope lies in my belief that God transforms us more often in our places of scarcity than in our places of abundance. I am assured, as I daily pray for these people suffering unimaginable pain, that in a year, or whatever is God's timing, the depths of their sorrow can be transformed into joy. I believe that!

There are now ten volunteer chaplains here for UMCOR and our nametags read CHAPLAIN. The state of NY has explicit rules about the use of the word "counselor". Besides, we are mostly WITH and listening TO those who wish to share. As we identified ourselves, many states were represented —California, Rhode Island, Western NY, Colorado, Florida, North Dakota, Delaware, Pennsylvania, Utah . . . The pastor from North Dakota said it was unbelievable to him that he could be in NYC on a record breaking 78-degree day—a hot day for October! He quipped, "It is a shock for my system to go from fifteen percent humidity to ninety percent humidity." Another chaplain smiled and said to him, "You might drown." Cute.

Everyone here in NY working with UMCOR is volunteering except one field staff member (coordinator) who is on stipend. Some conferences or churches or friends (like in my case) are helping with expenses, but our time is all donated and volunteered. No apportioned dollars go to UMCOR and One Great Hour of Sharing money is the only undesignated money that can be used for immediate emergency first response, to evaluate the need and set up for volunteers to come. This happens so soon after a disaster that it occurs before any other money can be collected. In the case of the WTC, UMCOR was up here setting up by Saturday, September 15, only four days after the tragedy, and as soon as routes were open into the city. Therefore, collected money (called Advance Specials) is spent for only the specific disaster, in the specific conference and goes directly to the vulnerable, fragile, and often hidden populations of people that fall between the cracks.

Igniting Ministry banners, the same ones Bill and I had carried with us and set up at all IM National Trainings for the last six months were picked up at one of the churches and distributed to all of the other downtown churches. Getting those big long boxes through the turnstiles of the subway stations presented an interesting challenge but, once hung, the banners were comforting, uniting reminders of whom we are called to be—with "Open Hearts, Open Minds, Open Doors." How perfect it is to see them hanging in the OPEN doorways of the nine Manhattan churches most severely affected by the terrorist attack. Whoever you are, whatever your situation, your challenge or your sorrow, we will listen and offer love and support. WOW . . . the people of the United Methodist Church. Only God's timing could have had the kickoff of that national ministry (and the new media blitz) be September 2001.

Some day I'll talk about the church service, Wonderful Wall Street Wednesday. Some day I'll talk about conversing with a pastor, about theology, who speaks only Japanese. We used a little machine that looks like a palm pilot. He would type in Japanese and I would read the words in English. I would type in English and he would read in Japanese. Amazing! He is going to start a new church service using one of the existing Methodist buildings. It will reach the young liberal inclusive Japanese population. We had much to share; the language barrier quickly became insignificant. Some day I will talk of the experiences of other chaplains. Some day I will debrief the group therapy session, which I attended (and needed to attend after this week) at Ground Zero. But now two experiences weigh heavy on my heart.

A man walked into the church right after work, about 5:45. perhaps he came from Wall Street. He looked fine in a power business suit, brown briefcase, wire-rimmed glasses, short hair kind of greased-back style, and likely in his early fifties.

He said, "I can't come to the session tonight, but I know that I need therapy. I'm just coming by to say that I'll be back. I KNOW I need therapy. But I'm on my way to Stanton Island tonight to another memorial service for a friend."

He told his story as if he were giving the review to a movie . . . non-emotional, just the facts ma'am, just the facts.

"I was trying to get out and had just gotten to the street, when the whole world turned black as midnight. I couldn't see where I was going . . . I was running, tripping over bodies and people trying to stand up . . . I slammed my head into a light pole, tripped over a fire hydrant or a parking meter . . . It was so dark. All I could do was blindly follow the noise of others running and we ran and we fell and we got up and we ran all the way across Brooklyn Bridge. That is the last that I remember until I woke up in the hospital . . . I had had a heart attack and an ambulance had picked me up. I didn't know until I woke up that the WTC buildings had collapsed. I didn't even know about the terrorist attack. I thought a bomb had blinded me. I didn't even know what was falling out of the sky. My body is healing, but the rest of me hurts. I need counseling and I just came by to say I'll be back."

Bless his heart . . . on his way to another memorial service!

I applaud him for knowing and telling the truth about himself. He needs help and is willing to say it out loud. I think that is the only reason he came by the church even though he couldn't stay . . . just wanted to say out loud what he knew in his heart he needed. Telling the truth to ourselves is a huge problem. Most of us lie about how much we eat or drink or watch TV or exercise or truly pray or read meditations. But those become white lies compared to major untruths we tell ourselves. Every time we blame another group or religion, or nation or even another person for some problem, we lie to ourselves about the role we play. Every time we gossip about someone else we lie to ourselves about why we do it. Each and every time we put someone else down for hair, looks, opinions, intelligence we lie to ourselves about our motives and intentions. We do these things to avoid looking at our own brokenness, our own needs, pains, and hurts. This man, having escaped from the WTC collapse, was forced to look at and acknowledge his. I do hope it will not require tragedy for the rest of us to see the truth—to thine own self be true and thou cannot be false to anyone.

I'm not a fire chaser, at all. So, in my week here, I had actually not been as close as I could get to the rubble and hole in the skyline left by the fall of seven of New York City's most prominent buildings. There appeared to be so many people in need outside the perimeter that I was satisfied that ministry could be done outside.

The white ash that covered my black shirt when I returned home at night saddened me. It was bizarre enough for me to blow my nose in the morning only to have the tissue blackened with ash and debris. But we were asked to walk the perimeter today. It was heart wrenching and I could do no ministry as I walked and cried. It is almost sickening to know what I call ash and debris, upon which we walk and that which we inhale into our lungs, includes cremains of over 5,000 human beings. The dust makes my eyes sting and the very thought of it leaves a permanent lump in my throat.

When the wind shifts, the smell is too pungent to describe. Yet, it is holy ground. Even after six weeks the area is somber. With each dump truck that passed I sobbed, not for the twisted, bent and broken steel, or the mangled conduits with cables twisted and torn, but for what each ton represented to us as a world. I wanted to thank the drivers for the job they are doing, but could barely make eye contact. The wound of September 11 is still open and raw.

Perhaps the most daunting of all pictures was that of several hundred black plastic bags stacked close to the barricade on the west side of the WTC site. At first I did not notice that they were all exactly the same size, yes, one-bucketful size. At first I didn't notice how gently the workers tossed them into the truck and stacked them one upon the other. At first I didn't hear the sound of stones gently hitting the bottom of the truck bed. At first I didn't see the tiny tear in a couple of bags allowing small amounts of contents to spill onto the sidewalk. At first I didn't realize that these bags were part of the crime scene and were being taken by truck over to Staten Island where each one would be sifted by forensic pathologists and checked for DNA. At first I didn't realize that two inches from my feet on that sidewalk were tiny particles of what was once human life, commingled, the innocent and the guilty.

I could do no ministry. I just looked at the workers and as our eyes met, I cried and they nodded. Why so many tears, Camille? You know and believe it is only the human house in which the spirit resided (for much too short a time.) But my heart still breaks for the needless act of violence . . . and for this act to be done in the name of religion is more horrific than I can even bear. Ashes to ashes, dust to dust.

A Pastor's Journal
Entry Nine - NYC - Ground Zero
October 25, 2001

As I awakened, through the open window drifted the aroma of roasted nuts with candy coating. My goodness, the vendors start early. I wonder how the odor can get up eleven floors, then find its way into my room through only a two-inch crack. (Thank goodness it is supposed to be a little cooler today.) Shift in the wind, I guess. But the window is great. I keep the window shade up all the way to the top during the night. Office buildings are directly across, with penthouse apartments on top. I can even see trees growing and plants blooming on the top of the building next to mine. With a little TLC anything can bloom where it's planted! I worry, however, about that office building being in plain view although a couple of blocks away. I have counted all of the floors . . .76. It looks so tall—so very vulnerable, especially at night, with a few lights on in random order on each floor. I wonder if those people are afraid.

I feel safe here in my room. That's interesting, because there are places where I don't feel safe. Not that I'm afraid anyone will break in or that I'll be hurt. It's just a nagging sense that the energy all around doesn't feel good. Hmmm, the peace lily has four new blooms today; must be good energy. New York City feels as safe to me as did our 10-acre 'farm' ('farm' used very loosely and if you ask the local people from Bahama, the word 'farm' to describe our ten acres would be a joke) right outside of Durham. Hey, we did raise rabbits, feed chickens, make cheese, can tomatoes, and I milked goats for the children's cereal every day. That sounds like a farm to me! Anyway, that's where the four of us were living when Randy died, and where I lived while I went to Divinity School. It was a great house. Two male students lived with us (downstairs, I mean) and we had a lot of divinity school parties there. The current Dean of the divinity school was in my graduating class. He says, "I'll promise not to talk about you, Camille, if you'll promise not to talk about me." So . . . I guess that's all I have to say about the house in Bahama.

The garage in New York, where I was keeping my car, (a very cheep price only for you) charged $25 a day, if I got the back of my receipt stamped by the hotel. So after three days, I moved my car to New Jersey.

The premise of the book Six Degrees of Separation is so very true. All across the world, within six relationships, someone will know someone who knows someone they know. It seems that the parents of my next-door neighbor in Raleigh live right outside of the city, because he is the principal oboist for the New York Philharmonic, and she plays with the New Jersey Symphony. So, not only did I have the opportunity to leave my car at their house for free, but I was blessed to be able to attend the Philharmonic at Lincoln Center with them.

During the ride in from NJ with two of the second violinists, the discussion centered around what it was like to have their car searched by police before each and every performance, even though they were assigned designated parking spaces under Lincoln Center. They said that even their instrument cases were searched before the performances. We passed a highly-guarded large complex-cement barricades, patrol cars, uniformed armed guards. What is that? I asked . . . "The water supply for New York City." Hmmm, it looked more like the Gaza Strip or the West Bank of the Jordan River. I remember being shocked in 1989 when I walked around Jerusalem's wall and saw many armed soldiers on guard guns. Now, here are our own soldiers guarding New York's water supply—I'm thankful they are.

While we listened to the beautiful pieces of Sibelius, Stenhammar and Beethoven, I was keenly aware that there were F-16s flying over (of course we couldn't hear them) protecting all of us from terrorist attack. They also flew that same night over Yankee stadium, as the "Bronx Bombers" were about to win the opportunity to go to the World Series. Experiencing both of these events while living in the midst of fear was quite emotional. "Do it afraid," as my dear friend Nancy says. All of must must "do it afraid," not just the families of the deceased affected, not just those who escaped the tragic collapse of the World Trade Center on September 11, but all of us.

I felt quite at home when I was with the symphony players. My little brother is the artistic director (conductor) of the Boise (Idaho) Symphony, where he lives with my dear sister-in-law and my two precious nephews. Now, what exactly is the likelihood that the oboe player of the New York Philharmonic—the father of my Raleigh next door neighbor, the baby sitter of my car while I do ministry for the disaster of the WTC—would have played in the same symphony that my brother conducted in Winston-Salem in summers during the 1970's? It's true. Maybe it should be less than six degrees of separation. With respect to the terrorist attack, it may be only two degrees—everyone knows someone who has been affected by the attack on the WTC. Sure we do, we just look in the mirror.

While waiting at the stage door after the concert for the players, I had a sense that the guard monitoring sixteen internal cameras had done the same before September 11. However, the bulletproof, electronically controlled, shatterproof glass door, which could only be opened from the inside, was new. Even with all that has happened music will survive; as the language of the soul, it will survive. Throughout history the arts have always survived.

I found out last night that the construction workers (not fire fighters or police) working in the rubble are in need of black steel-toed work boots, all men's sizes, any brand, as well as safety glasses, helmets, and work gloves. The debris is caustic, the steel difficult to walk on, and the workers are going through boots like crazy.

Ninety-five percent of all workers at the WTC site are Catholic. They very much appreciate carrying small crucifixes, rosaries, or medallions. It would be wonderful to have buckets full at the site for them to pick up for their daily shifts.

Art of a totally different style is surviving in *Wonderful Wall Street Wednesday*. This is the mid-week service and the only service for some. The workers take their lunch break to walk to the historic John Street UMC for the service. John Street is designed exactly like Evans Metropolitan Church in Fayetteville, where we celebrated unity and shared heritage (once again, I was proud to be a Methodist!) It was just about as hot today as in Fayetteville.

The preacher said, "We know you are on your lunch break. We'll keep OUR eyes on the clock . . . you keep your eyes on Jesus." We gave each other *high 5's—Jesus is alive*, and then more *high 5's—the Yankees won last night's game*. Hey, when in Rome, you do as the Romans.

This was ecumenism at work, co-sponsored by John St. UMC and Bronx Christian Fellowship. However, today's preacher was Hispanic, from the Assemblies of God Church. (This service was way out of the comfort zone for some UMCOR volunteers, but they did it anyway!) The choir was made up of mostly African Americans, but also included some Caucasians, Hispanics, and Asians. (By the way, UMCOR passed out the FEMA literature in New Jersey written in five languages, Hindu, Polish, Spanish, English and Arabic . . . way out in front of most of our provincial understanding of community)

The choir looked like the church of God on earth and, if not perfect in word or melody, it was perfect in spirit and LIVELY! The pastor said his wife called him a "Crazy Puerto Rican" for not being afraid. He told her that she knew he was crazy when she married him. And then he boomed, "Two Giants Have Fallen . . . Two giants of our Community have fallen, but the only true Giant has risen. God has risen in our midst. God has risen in our country. And God, the only giant, protects us from fear!" That will preach! Isaiah 41:17 God says, in effect, I will never abandon you, NEVER.

I do believe that. However, I am ministering now on the inside of the barricades where the workers are digging through the rubble intermixed with human remains (the hole they call it) and well, there are times . . . it's just hard. When an older man working within the barricades said, "I am a retired fireman, but I'm down here because my son is still in there." I could only weep.

A Pastor's Journal
Entry Ten - NYC - Ground Zero
October 26, 2001

I forgot to call home and check my messages. Home seems so far away. It was reassuring to talk to Rachel and Tyson today, my babies. Babies? 32 and 29. My two other babies are Cris and Julie (step children, but we NEVER say "step" and certainly don't feel it!) I talk to them several times a week as well. After all, we've been together as a family since the children were thirteen, fourteen, fifteen, and seventeen.

I am so glad they all are older now!!! Rachel and Tyson both called today, because they are flying, she to her annual meeting in San Antonio, Texas, and he to his annual meeting in Las Vegas, Nevada. Their calls were reassuring. I asked Rachel if she were afraid. She said, "No, Mom, however, I have called everyone I love just to tell them I love them, before getting on the plane." Yes, we as a nation are living more in the moment. After all, what choice do we have? I said, "Tyson, are you afraid to fly to Las Vegas?" He said, "No, well maybe apprehensive, but not afraid. It's not up to me to choose when it is my time to die, I'm just calling to say I love you." Words precious to my ears and words thousands of mourners here in NYC wish they could hear just one more time.

I will not take their words for granted. Rachel and Tyson both have learned valuable lessons about life in their brief years. Do I worry about them? NO! Worry is like rust on the blade of a saw: it only keeps you from being your best. I do wish, however, that all four children would have a faith community. They don't. They, along with their friends, come to me to discuss their theological questions, but that's not like being in community. Community is necessary. Some of your die-hard church people aren't necessarily your deeply spiritual persons, but they are needy. They are needy for community—Church becomes a way for them to connect on a deeper level with other human beings. They experience their emptiness and brokenness to a lesser degree when they share it within a like-minded, social-spiritual setting.

New York City is becoming more of a community. As I returned from the World Trade Center area on the subway yesterday, an older (older than I am, that is) African American woman, with several large bags, offered me her seat. I was stunned, but grateful, and said so. Nevertheless, I declined. In a few moments she and a few other passengers began talking to me . . . ON THE SUBWAY.

We were of different races, different ages, different socio-economic levels, as defined by our clothing, and coming from different places at the end of a long day at work, but we were all talking together. They had noticed my CHAPLAIN name tag (I had totally forgotten about it) and they saw the white breathing mask, dangling from my left wrist. It's unbelievable. I came up here to minister to these people and they ministered to me. Isn't that the way it always works? When we let it and perceive it! The woman had asked me if I wanted her seat because she said I looked tired. Another passenger said he could tell by the ash in my hair and all over my jacket, not to mention the mask, that I was just returning from the site. None of them had been down there.

They thanked me for coming to NYC to work with the victims and rescue workers of the terrorist attack. They thanked me . . . unreal. Then they asked how I was doing. I was totally overwhelmed (so overwhelmed in fact, that I missed my stop . . . by thirty blocks! No big deal really). We became a small community, right there on the Express Uptown Subway. We became like-minded human beings with a common denominator, in spite of our apparent differences. I accepted their ministry, even if I didn't accept the offer of a seat. That is community.

In Raleigh I am in a politically incorrect women's spiritual growth group. They are my community. I term us "politically incorrect" because of our name I guess. We call it CIC for "Chicks In Change." The name would probably offend the social and theological left wing, the liberals, because titles are important and the term "chick" is understood as a flippant, derogatory term for women. It could be perhaps perceived as taking a step backward in the liberation of women. On the other hand, the name offends the social and theological right wing, the conservatives, because the word "change" doesn't theologically signify any holy Christian principals. Tough! Isn't that what President George W. Bush did when he made the decision about disallowing certain studies on human embryos? I don't remember all of the facts, but I do remember that he offended both the left and the right. It seemed like a good decision to me. Anyway, CIC is a perfect name for us. We are diverse women, proud to be women. We meet weekly and are working on helping each other be transformed into more nearly perfect, whole, well, spiritual, complete, balanced, successful, joyful and healthy women. It is truly a supportive spiritual growth community. I love them. I let them support me and I let them challenge me. I let them teach me and they let me teach them. Without scholarly theories or intellectual language, I let them love me . . . the real me. We must be in good shape if we offend both sides of the social theological continuum.

Community is very apparent at Ground Zero. Family might be a more appropriate term. We learned that the toxic-fume level is higher. We witnessed an explosion or a fire of some sort. But that wasn't the only thing. The winds were high and had shifted (ahhh, the smell from the honey glazed roasted nuts in my window). Most people were walking around with coats or shirts or hands over their mouths and noses. The atmosphere was heavy and thick. Ash and debris were blowing around the site.

One chaplain told me of an event that happened as he was standing at one of the many pits the recovery workers are digging in the mass of rubble. He said a worker came out of the pit and excitedly told the group topside that they had found a body, then went back to help bring it out. The group stood in silence and reverence as the body came "out of the pit." All of a sudden, a whirlwind came swirling out of the hole encircling all standing there. The chaplain said it was a holy moment in his life—he felt as though he had been baptized with ash, through the holy wind. I thought to myself the term for Wind and Spirit and Breath, in both the Old Testament and the New are the same. In fact, I had used that as the premise for the Distinguished Divinity School Alumni Award I was blessed to present to Dr. A. Purnell Bailey last Monday at Duke. While I may be very far away from the grand halls of that magnificent university, the truth is the same. The chaplain was standing on holy ground and God was, and is, present in the wind and in the ash swirling around.

There is so much more to say but today my station is at a church as a listener counselor. I won't go back to WTC today. Under the circumstances, it would be difficult for my lungs two days in a row. In long conversations with military, from upstate NY, I learned that they, like me, were honored to be serving their twelve-hour-on, twelve-hour-off shifts. More about that later.

I worked inside of St. Paul's where the firemen, police officers, and constructions workers rest, eat and are refreshed. There I met the chaplain for the Catawba Police Department. You would have thought we were long lost friends. We hugged and chatted and talked about how very honored we were to be serving in this capacity. Some workers were asleep on the pews, others were eating soup ladled from large kettles and others were walking around the (unrecognizable) sanctuary, reading letters of love from a mourning nation. Some were getting massages, some having feet rubbed and Band-Aids applied. Some sat alone, head in hands. As I moved about, one of the firemen told me, "Yeah,

I pulled out two bodies today, firemen but I couldn't recognize anything." (Actually they were body parts.) He sounded numb and rather matter-of-fact. As we talked, I said something like, "You must be emotionally exhausted." He softly replied, "Oh . . . you get used to it." I think he is emotionally exhausted. We will spend more time together. I didn't cry at all today; hmmm maybe numbness for a time is a gift.

A Pastor's Journal
Entry Eleven - NYC - Ground Zero
October 27, 2001

The two of us were in the front seat of the car. My cell phone rang and I answered. Diane could hear only my part of the conversation because she was driving.

" Oh, hi . . . yes, it is only a month away, now. . . Oh that's right, sorry, it just slipped my mind . . . I will, but right now I'm on my cell phone and headed to an important appointment, but will e-mail you my resume and picture as soon as I get back to my office. I promise . . . Looking forward to it . . . Sure, great to talk to you, too. Thanks for calling. Bye"

Diane laughed, "That must have been from the big city where you are flying to teach the Igniting Ministry training next month."

"Yes."

"I bet he would get a big kick out of knowing that your really important appointment is Trish's bridal shower (in CIC group) and that your office consists of your make-up table where you keep your laptop." (Not true, I have my swivel-chair eye make-up table to the left and the computer to the right.)

This is the first time I have ever done any writing. I hate to write. But if I ever thought I might write, I envisioned a lovely cherry-paneled library with a disappearing computer cove, a thesaurus close at hand, all of my biblical reference books surrounding me, copies of old sermons filed very neatly, a secretary to take dictation (dream on), Will Willimon's theological anecdotes and illustrations at my fingertips, and one of those wonderful wooden ladders that runs along a track, so short people could reach tall shelves in an instant. However, as I sit down to write this I can only smile at such images. Right this minute, my laptop is on top of a fat NY telephone book, to help it be the right height; it's hanging off the edge to make room for the mouse pad. Three bottles of fingernail polish are sitting beside my laptop (foundation, color and quick dry, of course), along with a pen, small note pad, subway pass, curling iron, credit card, map of NY, and a zip-lock bag of today's vitamins. That might not seem too, too much, but this converted phone table is only eighteen by twenty inches. Bloom where you are planted; practice what you preach, Camille.

New York joke: What is the shortest measurable time in the universe? The time between the stoplight turning green and the horn honking behind you.

There has long been a controversy about ministry. There are denominations and pastors within denominations who believe clergy does it, clergy does ministry. The key word there is DOES. My take on ministry is that ministry is not what you do, but who you are. I have told all my churches that the only difference in my ministry and theirs is that I am ordained to WORD, ORDER, AND SACRAMENT. WORD, because my theological study, and successfully jumping through the hoops for ordination, give me the credentials to interpret the text and make it relevant to today. ORDER because through symbolic apostolic succession I have been given authority to order the life of the congregation and worship in particular. And SACRAMENT because the only two sacraments of the United Method Church, baptism and holy communion, must be carried out by ordained clergy. (Simplistic Methodist Discipline 101) Every other ministry is to be shared between clergy and laity. Do I have any more God-spirit in me than anyone else has when visiting the sick in the hospital? NO! Do I have anymore God-spirit in me when sitting beside the broken hearted? NO! Do I have any more God-spirit in me when being accepting and inclusive of ALL human differences? NO! Do I have any more God-spirit in being welcoming and making phone calls and visits? NO! ya da, ya da, ya da!

My boss Steve, in New Church Development, has said for years that the reason my churches have been so successful is that I delegate the entire ministry to the laity and don't do any of it myself. He is joking a little, but basically he's right. I do a disservice to any non-ordained persons by carrying out any form of ministry that they can do. Underneath my CHAPLAIN nametag, I'm just ordinary Camille. I'm doing nothing magic here in NY. In fact, there's nothing to DO. Our country has been devastated. But it's only a small piece of the tapestry. Each event in our lives is just a row of the tapestry that, viewed alone, cannot be understood and the picture cannot be seen. Put into perspective, however, looking at all of the previous rows and understanding that the tapestry is not finished and that there are many more rows to be sewn, only then can we begin to understand our particular row. In the recent terrorist attacks in New York, Washington DC, and Pennsylvania, we can only see one row . . . and we are looking at it from the knotty side, not the finished side. NO, there's nothing we could have done. So we must all stop feeling guilty for not being among those killed.

In general most normally healthy humans recover with or without help in the face of disaster. . . not without pain and struggle, but they recover. My ministry is just BEING ME, offering me. I have been invited to hold the hands of New Yorkers as they struggle with their recovery. Is there any more God-spirit in me while I hold their hand? NO. Wherever we each reside in this tapestry, there is a hand to hold. There is someone who needs the ministry of presence.

He just came in to use the restroom of the church. We are supposed to say that we don't have a public restroom. But he was huge, looked like a giant to me—handsome African American in a dark black suit—must have been almost six-foot-six, way over 300 pounds, but a gentle face. I noticed a coiled white wire running down his neck and into the collar of his starched white shirt. It was really noticeable because of his dark skin. I must have looked as if I didn't know the answer to his question about the rest room because I just stared at him for a second, stunned.

He said, "I'm police . . . Secret Service guarding Mike Green (candidate to succeed the mayor after Guillani) at the rally just across the street." He pointed to several black official cars that had pulled up in front of the church. I hadn't even noticed.

I said, "Of course . . . anything for the police," and gave him directions. He was back in a moment but the cars were all still just parked out there. He stayed and talked to me. We had the sign out that said listening center. All are welcome. Come talk about anything on your heart.

He relived his experience of September 11. He and his partner were in their car when the call came. They immediately responded, but were in upper northwest. Because of the terrible traffic, they didn't reach the scene before the buildings collapsed. As much as he fusses about the traffic, it saved his life that day. He and his partner were part of the first response team.

He said, "I should have been in that building with my friends."

"How many did you lose?"

"Personally, six that were good buddies. But I knew most of them. The fire fighters took the biggest hit. Some firehouses lost every single fire fighter. It is so sad."

I asked about his schedule. He told me, "It's better now. We were working twelve-on, twelve-off, seven days a week. We had a day off last week."

"How are you doing it, physically, emotionally?"

"It's my job, every person in NY is just as stressed out as I am. It is just so sad."

"Tell me how you take care of *you* in the midst of all of this."

He was silent for a moment. I noticed his lip quiver and big tears formed in his HUGE black eyes. Before they could run down his cheeks, he said, "I'm talking with you." With that, he got up and said, "Thanks for the rest room."

He walked out the door and got into the second big black official car parked in front of the church. As he was walking out, I wondered, "Did I DO any ministry or did I just hold a hand?"

After three straight hours of "listening," I stepped out of the Methodist Church in Greenwich Village. There on the steps sat a young girl. She was bent over a little, hiding the fact that she was sucking her thumb. I smiled to myself—Rachel sucked her thumb a long time, even though she was embarrassed. She would hide it under a blanket it when watching TV or even under a book when her head was down on her desk in kindergarten. I smiled at the young girl. She looked up, embarrassed too, that she had been 'caught.' She straightened up. Oh, my God. She's pregnant, eight or nine-months pregnant. Oh, my God. The CHAPLAIN name tag didn't help, I didn't know what to do . . . I just kept walking . . . faster. Oh, my God, Oh, my God, who is holding that child's hand?

A Pastor's Journal
Entry Twelve - NYC - Ground Zero
October 28, 2001

I called my webmaster today and said, "Jack, I just can't write any more. I'm not sleeping. These stories keep running around in my head and all the people I talk to are in my mind constantly. So I've got to stop writing because I just can't sleep."

In his very calm manner (He and his wife are both nine's, I'm a seven on the enneagram) he replied, "Camille, I don't think it's the writing that is keeping you awake. It's the stories themselves. You're dealing with so much concentrated grief." DUH! Of course. Everybody grieves differently. I can't sleep.

One evening, in 1980, I was standing on a step stool in the hallway of the house in Bahama, painting the wall. The telephone rang (this is as clear to me as if it were yesterday). It rang and rang and rang. There was no such thing as as answering machine or voicemail or caller-ID. The phone probably rang fifteen times. I finally got off my step stool, put my hands on my hips, and complained (probably quite loudly) as I walked, "Do I have to do everything around here? Couldn't someone answer the phone?"

The children were only seven and nine. As I walked into the den, there sat Randy in his big chair, with both children in his big lap—all three had tears running down their faces. He said, "I'm sorry I didn't answer the phone. I couldn't talk, we're watching *Little House on the Prairie."* Did I ever feel insensitive! But that's who Randy was. He still had his grand football size, left over from playing at Manlius Military Academy and Syracuse University, but not his athletic physique. Nevertheless, everyone knew what a teddy bear he was. He was the "roll around on the floor with the children" and "make up the bedtime stories" kind of guy (Tyson is just like him).

Back then I was taking orientation classes to acquire the skills to answer the Crisis telephone lines for Contact Teleministry in Durham. In preparation for dealing with extreme grief on the crisis lines, we were studying the writings of Elizabeth Kubler Ross. She was at Duke at the time and was then the authority on death and dying. On Tuesday night of this particular week, we had studied the stages of grief. These stages aren't linear but include shock, denial, bargaining, anger, overwhelming sadness, emptiness, and finally acceptance (That's about the best I can do from memory—where's that cherry-paneled library with the wooden ladder that runs along the track)?

Most people in the midst of grief vacillate among them on their journey toward recovery—sort of two steps forward, one step back. I remember that fateful day when I was forced to experience the stages of grief. I didn't realize until Friday morning that Randy had not come home from a late meeting Thursday night. After calling the police and the hospitals, I stood on the porch in a state of panic and watched as my dear neighbors Tom and Linda drove up. They leaped from their car and came running up the front walk towards me. They were both frantic. Tom was saying, "There has been an accident," and Linda was hysterically repeating, "He's dead, Camille. He's dead, Camille. Camille, he's dead!"

From their words and body language, I knew immediately what they were trying to tell me, even as I denied it. I ran toward them screaming "No, no, no, it can't be true." Then, "Oh, please, please, don't tell the children." It seems strange to remember this, but even as those words came out of my mouth my brain was repeating, shock and denial, shock and denial. "Camille, you are in shock and are denying what they just told you." The grief process was just beginning.

Here in New York, people are experiencing all stages of that grief process. Some still can't believe the United States has been attacked by terrorists. Others choose not to. A Gen-X Asian woman told me about coming down from her 25th-floor office building only to see the people in her area, toward midtown, silently walking toward the bridge. There was no public transportation—everything had been immediately shut down.

She said, "We were like cattle, each following the one in front of us, slowly, no panic. We had no news of what was happening, no phone service, no communication whatsoever. Hours later, as we crossed the bridge, I could not look toward the Twin Towers. I could not look at the skyline at all. Here it is six weeks later and I still can't look. I'm not grieving or having any trouble with grief; I just still can't look at the skyline."

She thought she wasn't grieving, but she did come in to talk. We discussed her actions in relation to the various stages of grief and concluded that she was progressing in the grieving process, perhaps being still in denial. She needed to know that the other stages would be just as normal, whenever they come, and that they would come when time was right for her.

A Gen-X student at Union Theological Seminary said he just went about his work in his protected environment. He says he uses trite religious phrases to sustain him and has not felt anything yet. Our talk about the stages of grief led to the conclusions that he is still in a stage of shock. Only when he is ready will he let the pain in and then be able to progress toward healing.

One young gay man had just moved to New York two weeks before the events and was ecstatic about having an interior-decorating job in Midtown. He found out about the terrorist attack when his mother called him at work from "out west." She called, frantically telling him, "Get out, get out." He said he almost didn't accept her call because she worries so much about him being in the big city. She calls him all to often. He is in the sadness stage—an outpouring of tears that seem never to stop. It's impossible for him to look at fabrics and colors. He feels his whole world has turned to grays and blacks. Overwhelming sadness colors his world. We talked about the stages of grief. He is fine where he is right now, and color will eventually come back into his world.

A Caucasian middle-aged, quite radical man, who fought in Vietnam, fuses and cusses about the blankety-blank CIA, FBI, the Senate, the House, Congress, and all government agencies that obviously knew that this terrorist attack was about to happen and didn't do anything, didn't warn us. If only they had told the air traffic controllers, ya da, ya da. If only we had been told the truth, this anthrax thing wouldn't have gotten out of hand. "Those lying so-and-so's." (This one was harder for me to listen to.) We also discussed the various stages of grief. He is in the bargaining stage: if we had only—if they had only. I'm not sure I got through to him about the various stages (perhaps some drug damage there). He may stay in this bargaining stage for a long time; however, if he is ever to reach acceptance, he must progress through other stages. He may not experience all of them, but he will pass through most of the stages of grief. Some people tell me they never got angry when going through their stages. My personal opinion is that they just didn't perceive their feelings as anger.

There was a woman in the elevator who was in a wheelchair. I said, "Good morning," and she started talking. She asked me who I was and why was I staying in the Habitat Hotel. I showed her my badge.

She said in a bitter way, "I guess you won't talk to me. I live here."

"Of course I will." I replied, "Here's my card." (It just has my name, Hope in the Wilderness, and my cell phone number.)

She called me three times before I had time to go to her room the next evening. She greeted me at the door (no wheel chair) in nothing but an old dirty long tee shirt. But her nails were bright red and about an inch longer than her fingers. Her hair (blond the last five inches and solid gray the five inches closest to her head) was long for her diminutive but busty body. She was quite feisty and intelligent, and appeared to have "been around" in her day.

The tiny room in which she had lived was cluttered beyond belief. It was difficult for me to get in the door because of all of the stacks and piles of debris. Hoarding boxes and papers and magazines and clothes and anything else hoardable, she had only one clean spot—her tiny twin bed. She made her way to the twin bed and got in it as she talked. I made my way through the maze, stepping through the clutter, and sat in a broken chair at the end of the bed, on top of a stack of newspapers. My feet were resting on recently received QVC packages not yet opened.

I once again felt guilty for fussing about my room (which I now know had obviously been remodeled) for hers was much worse. The stark white plaster was cracked and fragments had fallen from the walls and ceiling. Her room was the same size as mine but in hers, stacks of hoarded goods loomed around us. She had a chest of drawers with no knobs, a tiny refrigerator, and she must have had a microwave, because she asked me if I wanted any hot tea. I thanked her but declined.

Immediately upon entering, I had been reminded of news clips of eccentric people dying in homes filled to the ceiling with stuff. She related stories of her nephews in medical school and nieces who were dancers on Broadway. She told of being knocked down on the day after the attack by dark-skinned, turbaned men running through the streets yelling, "Death to Americans." I listened to the woes of living in a terrible place like this with all of the homeless people that the government was paying to let them live here. I nodded as she told of the hotel filling up the floors with the people who were displaced from the WTC Community after the "bombing." "Of course the hotel was lying about all of those people losing their homes because of terrorists." She was sure they were just homeless getting to live in her hotel for free. She was angry with her grocer, her doctor, the hotel, and the Muslims. After about an hour she stopped and got very serious. She said, "I am so sorry for telling you all of this. I just don't know what is wrong with me. I am angry about everything. I'm just not like this, really I'm not. I love New York." Everybody grieves differently.

We talked about the stages of grief. She is definitely in the anger stage. I told her that no matter how she is feeling, it is OK for now and that life as she had known it would eventually return. (Only time will tell how normal that might be in her case.) We talked for a very long time.

Finally, I said, "I need to go now. Can I do anything for you? Is there anything you need?"

"No, I'm just fine."

She got out of bed and walked me to the door, but we couldn't find space to stand too close together. I placed my feet between some stacks, leaned over, and hugged her, a full big hug. For the first time that night, tears came to her eyes.

She said, "Thank you. That's what I needed."

It was what I needed as well.

A Pastor's Journal
Entry Thirteen - NYC - Ground Zero
October 29, 2001

Here in New York City, I find it harder to pray. I normally pray for about thirty minutes as soon as I wake up. Here, it now takes over an hour because I can't seem to stay focused or even stay in a meditative state. The magnitude of ministry to be done and the pain of individuals creeps in with every breath I take. I also find it difficult to maintain a schedule for reading my daily meditation books. (At home they stay in my bathroom, here . . . well)

Maybe my prayers are supposed to change while I'm here. Maybe I should just continue to ask for blessings to be able to do whatever God has for me to do, to be free from evil, to cause no pain, and to allow the light to shine through me. Maybe I should just continue giving thanks for each system in my body that allows me to still be alive, well, and working! Maybe I should just leave it at that. Maybe I don't need to surround in the light each and every person that I love, or pray for his or her highest and best good for today in God's plan. Or maybe that would be a cop-out. It is hard to discern right now. It's just not as easy to pray . . . hmmm, doesn't it seem that it should be easier to pray up here???

One of my favorite colleagues from North Carolina said today, "Well, Camille, you DO march to the beat of a different drum." I replied that I don't do it on purpose. It's not a form of rebellion; it's just that I feel the beat of the drum so intensely that sometimes I think I will explode. I guess right now I'm at the explosive level. I am pained by another North Carolina colleague who has carried out a writing campaign against the Igniting Ministry (I.M.) program. He has opposed this work in letters to bishops, in e-mails across the denomination, in letters to conference newspapers and in other media. While I respect his right to his opposing viewpoint, this condemnation nonetheless pains me. I don't think I'm hurt because I.M. was my "baby" for seven months (Oh, I do hope not!) and that I was a national trainer to help churches prepare for "Open Hearts, Open Minds, and Open Doors" and the media blitz. I don't think so. But who knows the human psyche? It could be.

This man's premise, and that of those within his theological group, accuses I.M. (and the Methodist Church really) of not offering Jesus Christ, not preaching repentance of sins, and not teaching death and resurrection. The I.M. program has its purpose to reach the unchurched, primarily those between 25 and 54 years of age. For the most part, these people do not respond to traditional Christian words and phrases (Neither do a lot of boomers, by the way.) I.M. appeals through the media in less traditional, but theologically sound, methods. My question is (and I'm no theological genius!), should we offer the name on the birth certificate of Jesus, the height of the historical Jesus, his weight, the color or length (for goodness sake) of his hair, or perhaps proof of his gender (hmmm, that's another issue)? Is it actually the DNA of Jesus that he wishes we would offer? Or is it the spirit of the Christ, alive and well within each human spirit, if awakened and offered to another human being—that spirit of love offered freely and without reservation? Oh sure, it's expressed differently, but then all human beings must eat food in order to live and, when given the opportunity, will choose different items from the menu or even different restaurants in which to eat. In the end, it's the food which nourishes, and so it is with spiritual food.

At a time such as this, (with the terrorist attacks so fresh in our minds; with the media warning us that within the week there will be more attacks; and with possible attacks using anthrax, which destroys without discrimination as to race, gender, preference, or religious creed), it is tolerance of differences that will unite us. Whether aware or unaware, every (non-pathological) human longs for, and is in fact lured by, the loving creator who makes all things new again. Each human spirit longs for an eraser for the past—an eraser for past pains, shortcomings, and brokenness. Each longs for a spirit within to make the todays and tomorrows more nearly whole and joyful than the yesterdays. Nevertheless, food for the human spirit is served a different spiritual "restaurants," and even at the same restaurant, we may be fed different items from the "menu." In the end, all spiritual food nourishes, unless spoilers, such as Bin Laden, have poisoned it.

Death and resurrection are nowhere more apparent than in New York City. Just beyond the ashes of the WTC, and even among the ashes, new life springs forth. New hope and the spirit of a new day are working together. Muslim beside Christian, Jew beside Buddhist—all faiths are working side by side with those who have not yet found a path upon which to travel. I am responsible only for how the light shines through me—even that is a gift! We have an incredible opportunity for coming out of the darkness of the tomb and into the radiant light of a new holy day. Out of the horror of September 11, a new day is dawning.

I am embarrassed that we stand behind statements such as, "repent of your sins." First of all, the subject of that demand is the word YOU. Yet repentance can only start with ME. A man from AA shared with me his feeling that when he's in church the preacher is separated from him—way up there in the pulpit—preaching about what those in the congregation should do, while in AA they sit in a circle and experience life together. The good, the bad and the ugly experiencing life together sounds like one beggar helping another beggar find food.

I am distressed that we don't explain that one definition of the word sin is derived from an archery term that means to miss the mark, and one definition of "repent" comes from a word meaning to turn around and take a new path. (Duh . . . this path is killing me, and those around me; so, I'll turn around and won't follow this path any more!!!!) Here in New York, I've had several opportunities to deal with Gen-Xers who feel their life is missing the mark. (No, they didn't use those words.) They are successful Gen-Xers who offer to buy my lunch, if I will just spend time helping them move beyond this place in their life to another. Excuse me, but that sounds to me like "missing the mark, turning around and taking a new path!!" The terrorist attack on the World Trade Center has opened the hearts and minds of millions of people to the opportunities for reevaluating their lives and for turning around and taking new paths. The Christ-spirit is alive and well in NYC.

One beautiful, elegant woman in her mid-forties shared that her husband (mid-fifties) was having an affair with his secretary, a situation that devastated her. She cried over the embarrassment she felt in the grocery store when she saw friends. (She was sure everyone knew.) She said she was so humiliated that she didn't want to go to church anymore. She admired Hilary for how she had handled the Monica Lewinski situation. This woman had put up with his actions for years; he had moved out four times but always begged to come back. Their teenage children were beginning to hate him.

When the terrorist attack occurred, she had said, "Surely, he will get it through his head that life is short and that he needs to be with his family—his faithful wife of 20 years, and his teenage children, the girl in college." We discussed how the WTC event is not about HIM, but about her, about how it is going to affect her response to the marital situation. This is her opportunity to reevaluate her position, to turn around and take a new path. However, it is a frightening place to be. It is difficult not blame the behavior of someone else for our lack of happiness. It's easier to blame our parents for our dysfunctional family system (who doesn't have one???) It's easier to blame a boss, a spouse, a child, a pastor, or a traumatic event.

The difficult thing for this woman, just like for the rest of us, is to look to herself to see where SHE has missed the mark (not in taking blame, but perhaps in being too tolerant). Now, with the shakeup from the WTC event, she has an opportunity to take a new path.

One young man, aged thirty, (the exact age of my son, Tyson) is so very hungry for a new path. I've seen and talked to him twice. He's tall, thin, attractive, and with hair that he spikes up on top of his head (probably with mousse, as Julie and Rachel do theirs). He is successful, artistic, and musical.

A few days after the terrorist attack, his significant other walked out. She had lots of reasons (she said), but regardless of her reasons, he is devastated. He is especially overwhelmed because her leaving has only added to the pain of his losing many friends in the collapse of the WTC buildings. His grief is profound, and yet he feels guilty about his grief, knowing the gravity of everyone else's losses in New York. He grieves openly, and the incidents of the past few weeks have caused him to reevaluate his whole existence—his schedule, his coping strategies, his social life, his escape mechanisms, and the women he chooses to love (traumatic events have a tendency to cause us to reevaluate). The best thing is his hunger for change.

Together, we worked out a covenant for him to do the work. He made a list of his 20 best accomplishments of the past twelve months (from Cheryl Richardson's book), even though it was uncomfortable and difficult for him. He made a list of his behaviors that keep him from being the person he wants to be, such as staying out too late, not getting enough sleep, drinking too much, watching too much TV. It was discomfiting for him to make this list. He discovered the symptoms that show when he is out of balance (dishes piled up in the sink, no clean clothes, clutter all around, not going to work out at the gym). He was then willing to pick something over which he had control and which he was willing to change for one week. He did it!!! Talk about recognizing when you have missed the mark and then turning around and taking a new path. It's a huge start. He feels better. I am blessed to be in NY and to have the opportunity to meet people where they are, to take their hand, and to walk with them as they journey. This is not a quick fix, but merely the first step on a transformational journey. It doesn't feel as though I'm marching to the beat of a different drum. It feels like the only drum.

Daily, I am concerned with the vastness of the ministry opportunities in NYC and the little I feel that I accomplish in any one day; then I remember the one starfish the man saved when he couldn't save them all. If I have done anything to ease the pain of that one young man, it is important work. I wish someone had done the same for my son.

A Pastor's Journal
Entry Fourteen - Home Again
October 31, 2001

I slept eleven hours in my own bed. My body is back in Raleigh, NC, but my heart is still with the people of New York.

I can't get the young Vietnamese doctor out of my mind. He's an intern at St. Vincent's. He couldn't talk much about his work. He stared down at his hands and just shook his head slowly. St. Vincent's is the hospital closest to the World Trade Center and the place where most of the ambulances first went.

What can be done for him? What can ever erase the sights, sounds, and smells he has experienced? What can ever take away the helpless feeling he had as he watched, in revulsion, the horror of the terrorist attack? He said little, not wanting to betray the privacy, the confidentiality, of his patients. I thought of the irony of his situation. He's not old enough to have experienced the horrors of the war in Vietnam, although I'm sure he has heard family stories. Then he came to the USA for a better life—now this!

Once again, the affirmation overwhelms me: There is no safe place but within. When he left, I worried that he felt exactly the same as when he came in. I was unable to help him. In truth, only he can deal with the horrors he has experienced.

Another man who talked to me is Irish. I can't get him out of my mind. His name was "O'Something," and there was a strong hint of faded red in his gray hair and beard. His bright-green eyes sparkled with life and vitality. He was a proud carpenter and was wearing work clothes when I talked to him. His tears revealed his often overwhelming sadness, but he didn't seem embarrassed. He said he had been sober for sixteen years, 51 weeks.

I automatically said, "How fabulous to have been sober for seventeen years."

He immediately corrected me. "No, I still have eight more days to go. Every day is a new day, a new opportunity to make choices." (Wow! Once again, who was ministering to whom?)

He works at New York University and his AA group meets down near the WTC (He lives in a borough outside of the city and he explained how all the five boroughs make up greater NYC.) So, for almost seventeen years he has met with mostly the same guys; lots of young ones had started coming. He told of the numbers of young ones who had started coming and of the significant changes in AA. There is no smoking in the buildings anymore, and that's good for him, he noted, because he doesn't smoke or drink coffee. He's an athlete, albeit a middle-aged athlete.

In his words, he said, "Now, those sons-of-bitches have terrified our country and killed over half my AA group."

It's an indescribable loss for him. I immediately recalled how close I am to the seven other women in my CIC group after only one year. How very devastating it must be for him. Every man who died was younger than he is. He had sponsored several of them and feels like a parent who's lost his children. Oh my God, how widespread is the pain from this disaster!

He explained to me that AA is his church. I told him I understand and commented that I ask every pastor I mentor and nearly every person I counsel if they know anyone who is an alcoholic. If the answer is "yes," and it usually is, I suggest that they go to Alanon. They rarely go. He nodded, knowingly. I continued that probably they don't want to be seen at such of a meeting because to them there is a stigma attached. He nodded again. I told him it's the best program I have ever seen (especially for a nominal donation per meeting) to get one's own act together and to stop blaming the rest of the world. He nodded again. (Why was I telling him this?)

Adamantly, he said, "Alanon is good, but nothing compared to AA." I nodded.

He shared a story about a "real" church. Once, a pastor was trying to get the point across that we owe God our best. He told the congregation to come back on Wednesday night for a feast, dressed in their finest to prove to God that they would "give Him" their best. So on Wednesday night my friend presented himself at the church dressed in new blue jeans, no holes, with his grandfather's ruler in his back pocket, a clean and lightly starched blue work shirt, his best flannel jacket, and brand-new work boots. But they didn't let him in, because he didn't have on a suit and it was a "dress up" dinner for God. Of course, he was hurt. He said, "Didn't that preacher guy know someone else who was a carpenter? Hey, that carpenter's clothes didn't look that great to me."

AA is his church. I'm not surprised.

He said to me, "You don't act much like a preacher." I knew he meant it as a compliment.

I said, "Thank you, thank you very much!"

I have memories of a Hispanic woman telling me how, on September 11, she ran for two and a half hours from the store where she works on the upper East Side, all the way down to the area of the WTC. Her fourteen-year-old son was in school just a few blocks away. Her eyes misted as she relived the panic of that time and the fear of not knowing that he was fine. When she found him, the two of them then ran another two and a half hours back to the upper West Side to get her baby, who was staying with the grandmother.

I have memories of a young Asian woman, in the John Street neighborhood, who heard the noise on September 11 and looked out her door, only to see a large cloud coming down the street, "just like in one of those sci-fi movies." She couldn't believe she didn't die. She still has nightmares, but worries more about her husband who had been caught even closer than she to the chaos. He seems immobilized by the memories, unable to move on with his life.

My memories of the Memorial Wall on the west side of the WTC are much too vivid. The Memorial is adjacent to one of the piers on the Hudson River. In my personal and professional life, I have been faced with loss, death, and grief. I still affirm that each life lost represents family and friends grieving, and that the circumstances can add to the pain. The difference between the losses I have experienced and witnessed in the past and the recent experiences in New York is the shear enormity of the losses in New York. While each individual loss is no greater or less than that felt by others under similar conditions, the losses are cumulative and have affected and continue to affect millions of people.

To walk the wall is to see flowers stacked several feet deep the entire way. There's a flower shop on almost every corner in Manhattan for some reason, possibly because there is little greenery. At any rate, people have bought bunches of flowers wrapped in plastic and have continued to stack them on top of each other so that the freshest ones are on the top. The flowers have formed a wall of their own. Memorials to almost 6,000 people—it's immeasurable!

There are thousands of pictures also. Some are encased in plastic; others are in frames. Many are in the form of posters. There are letters from spouses, parents, friends, and children.

One letter reads, "Mommy and Daddy, we will miss you, but Grandmommy will take good care of us."

One is a large anniversary card with a picture of the bride and groom above it. It says, "Happy first anniversary, Sweetheart." The date is the day I was reading it.

Pictures are not to be taken at this site. When I wasn't crying myself, I put my hand on the shoulder of someone who was sobbing, or passed out tissues, or asked people please to respect the wishes of the families and not take pictures. There are many signs posted requesting no photographs "By order of the NYPD."

The police and fire memorial is on the other side of the sidewalk and a little closer to the river. It is under a tent and, like the Memorial Wall, has all kinds of personal memorabilia—teddy bears, candles, baseball gloves, rosaries, Yankees ball caps, champagne glasses. Thousands of innocent people gone, and millions experiencing grief—in my mind, this is the saddest point in the history of our country to date.

I will have forever etched in my memory the bizarre picture of talking to the police and National Guard at the site where the trucks come in and out of the barricade. They all wore HAZMAT facemasks, and I had on my white breathing mask. We looked like Martians. We wore our protective masks faithfully, however, because it has been discovered that the lungs of many of the workers at the site contain particles of dust that is composed of cement, asbestos, steel, and glass.

No wonder our eyes burn and we find it difficult to breathe. Each truck is power-washed inside the fence before it passes through the gates to come outside. This is done to contain the caustic contaminants inside the barricade as much as possible, and to prevent them from being released into the streets of New York.

The light mist that blew from the water hoses and hit my skin was sometimes refreshing and sometimes chilling, but always a distressing reminder of where I was standing. With a shiver I realized once again that everyone in the area treats the site as holy ground and that here there is also an overwhelming sense of patriotism (Two drivers had on American flag bandanas.)

There is much to be said for being washed off. I am at home now, and I am deeply grateful for my bed, my flowers, my dog and cat, my fresh air, my family, and my life.

I will be physically away from the destruction of the World Trade Center for one week. I will return next week. I will have twelve-hour shifts at St. Paul's, where I will serve however they need me, with the firefighters, police, construction workers. I will be confined to that one space for twelve hours. In the meantime, I am washed off and free from contaminants, physically and emotionally. I will get a second wind; then I shall return to that holy ground.

I am thankful for all who have supported my ministry financially and by reading my journal. Many blessings to them

—may they cherish what they have, who they are and those whom they love.

A Pastor's Journal
Entry Fifteen - NYC - Ground Zero
November 9, 2001

No, the detox center was not for drugs or alcohol, but to rid my body of harmful toxins stored in cells and especially in the colon. Well, that was the physical reason I went, anyway. I came home a year ago today. My friend Lois from Divinity School flew from NY to take care of me for a week, since the detox had made me pretty weak.

Linda was the director of the center. One of the many important things that she taught me was about my body. In my fragile state I cried often (surprise, surprise). She asked me if I thanked my body. Of course not! I hate my body . . .always have. It's never tall enough, always too fat, (and worse now than ever) with a rear end that will never fit into normal-size clothes. I sobbed crying, "What about my body is there to thank?"

In her gentle, sweet voice, she said, "Camille, can't you thank your lungs for breathing all the time you are yelling at me? Can't you thank your heart for beating while at the same time your eyes look at the beautiful fall colors outside? Can't you thank your stomach for digesting all of the stuff you put in it and for turning it into energy and knowing what you need and don't need? Can't you thank your most important colon for getting poisons out of your body? Can't you thank your white cells for rushing to a wounded site and healing it?" Oh, my gosh, I had never thought of any of that.

What a spoiled brat I had acted like all of my life. How arrogant it is in fact to think that everyone in a room is concentrating on how many pounds I might have gained or lost in any given day. Here I was a person who claimed to be positive, while all the time looking at the negative aspects—the unimportant exterior— ignoring the magnificent, God-created machinery that was doing its best to take care of me. From that day forward, hmmm a year now, I have started my prayers, every day, by thanking each system in my body.

Actually I start by thanking my hair. This sounds superficial, even stupid, but when you've always heard that your hair looked better the way it was before (no matter how it looks today) and when chemo ravages what you have, even if you don't loose it, I decided it was important to just thank it. I thank my eyes for seeing the gorgeous, full, unbelievably huge orange moon as I ride in the car with my son. I thank my nose for the odor of dry leaves blowing into my open bedroom window . . . and so it goes throughout every system in my body every day. Linda helped me be grateful for the physical house in which my spirit dwells in this life.

This first day back in NY, however, I am having a hard time being grateful. In my un-vacuumed room (what kind of diseases do you get from un-vacuumed hotel rooms?), there are no towels, no wash clothes, no pillows, no blanket (not that I would need it . . . the hotel always seems hot). My "suitemate" this time is a boy in his twenties. All day and all night there is constant traffic—male, female, several different races. At least he's inclusive. It's quite a stretch for me to act unaffected when, wearing my nightgown, I run into them in the hall. There's no stopper in the sink, but I decided just to take a sponge bath in my room today (This can't go on forever). Then, too, the mirror is broken, which seems to me is bad luck. There must be, correction, there IS a lesson for me here somewhere! Be flexible, Camille, you have clean sheets. Oh, how I wish I had brought my own pillow . . .but on the airplane?

I spent some time with two Gen-X men from Switzerland. One works for Novartis Pharmaceuticals, a really nice fellow who spoke very little English. He was able to tell me, however, that the cheese in America "sooks," it really "sooks." "WE, GOOD CHEESE." The other young man works for the Bank of Switzerland. It seems they came over to show their respects to Americans. "NO, turban man is going to hurt the best country in the world without us trying to help. We are spending our money to help the United States." He made a side comment: "American girls think we are cute and it doesn't matter whether we speak good English or not!" I can relate to that!

On the day of September 11, the banker was sitting at his three monitors at work and the live broadcast came on. "We couldn't believe a plane could make such a mistake and hit the World Trade Center in America. We thought it was a joke on us. Then we were watching as the second plane hit the other building. At that moment I knew the world had changed. I was connected to the World Trade Center by computer. Seventy-five employees of the Bank of Switzerland died in that building that day. Those bastards did that to us, not just to you." We talked about their grief. He said that for the first time in its history his company stopped all business. It stopped all business for ten minutes. Many people cried. The Novartis man could obviously understand more than he could speak. He nodded and looked solemn. We hugged just before parting, and I had a feeling that they perhaps appreciate what we have in America a lot more than we do.

I met again with the young man who was on vacation on September 11. He should have been on the 104th floor of WTC. This young man had lost all his friends and his mentor. His company is floundering as it tries to put itself back together. He's been trying to set up computers, reestablish the client base, deal with the grief of all of the clients, deal with the grief of all of the family members of his close friends, and deal with the grief he feels about his whole life. He's been to over 20 memorial services and he's not finished yet. Oh how sad for those families. He is as overwhelmed as any person I have ever seen. The sad truth is, when one point in a system changes, the entire system changes. Everything in his life is different. He is out of toilet paper and deodorant, hasn't had time for a hair cut, and received over 20 cell phone calls in the two hours we spent together, most of which he didn't even answer. I don't think he has followed up with the counseling referral I gave him.

I tried to help him get organized. I said let's write some things on your day timer (calendar).

He said, "My day timer was blown to bits in the World Trade Center. It had my whole life in it and I just haven't been able to get another one."

I told him that I have money to help him. My friends and their churches are paying my expenses here, giving money to be spent at my discretion. They would be glad for some money to be spent to help him get some rest—a massage, a day at a spa, or whatever would be of help.

He said, "No, your friends need to spend their money on the families of the victims, not on me."

Bless his heart; he doesn't even know what a victim he is. He did put the list we made in his pocket.

He told me that yesterday, with about $10 million in trades sitting on his desk, the loud speaker boomed, "There has been a bomb threat . . . get out if you want to." Most everyone left. The upper levels of traders, whose lives depend on second-to-second trading, stayed a couple of minutes. Then they looked at each other and said, "This is stupid." They evacuated the building while the elevators were still running. It took over an hour for swat teams and bomb squads to declare it safe to return. Then at three p.m. there was a second evacuation announcement, "GET OUT, EVERYBODY, GET OUT NOW, NO ELEVATORS RUNNING." Employees ran down as many as 35 flights of stairs of the newly-rented building, all panicked, all with the too-dramatic pictures of the

WTC in their mind. Nothing exploded, except a whole day's work—a day's work lost.

He went home, he said, "with the flu." He threw up all night. I don't think it was the flu. There didn't seem to be any words of wisdom from me. I'm not sure I was even helpful. What is there to do for this 31-year-old man? How much more can he take?

As I say my prayers, giving thanks for all systems of my body, I give thanks that I have a heart that keeps on beating, all the while it is really breaking.

A Pastor's Journal
Entry Sixteen - NYC - Ground Zero
November 10, 2001

My other room had a clock. This one doesn't but it does have
a TV with a channel flipper. It is quite hard to hear the TV
because of the street noise. Hmmm, without a TV, last trip I
didn't even notice the loudness of the street noise. There is
no mattress pad (that's scary) and the lampshade is hanging on
by a thread (actually it's tape), and mostly there is just wire
showing. I hear a strange hissing noise coming off of the floor
near the window. Could it be steam heat? God, I promise I will
not take so much of my life for granted, I promise.

Funny, the Swiss men both thought it was worth coming to
American just to eat the meat.

The banker said, "The cows, the Swiss cows, they crazy or
something."

I think he referred to mad cow disease; anyway they love
American meat. When I told them I didn't eat meat and was
mostly vegetarian, they thought I was crazy (must be a word
they knew).

The other one, not the banker, said, "It's like Italian not like
spaghetti . . . ha ha."

They are so cute .

Last week while I was at home, a newspaperman came to interview me about the journal.

He asked an interesting question, "Didn't you take a course in Divinity School that gives you the answers to questions like Why did God let this happen? Don't you have answers to give these people in New York? We expect pastors to have answers, you know." He was quite serious.

Oh, dear, maybe I was absent that day. I must have been absent the whole week when they handed out all of the answers to life's questions. I know I should probably be able to quote appropriate Biblical texts to give the answers to people's grief, pain, hatred and unfair life situations. But how can they hear unless they have a living relationship with that text? I might as well quote from Pilgrim's Progress (not that I could.)

Maybe most pastors do have the answers and can quote them but I can't. I can offer hope through my presence and MY belief in the triumph of good over evil. I am a living example that all of life goes through stages of brokenness and restoration, just like the Biblical texts, i.e. creation—good/the fall—bad; the flood—bad/dry land—good; wandering in the wilderness—bad/the promised land—good; crucifixion— bad/ resurrection—good. It's the story of all of life: everybody's, mine, and the people to whom I speak in New York. No magic words, just the ebb and flow of life's cycle over millions of years—with the ultimate triumph of good over evil.

I told my daughter, Rachel, about his question. She said, "It makes sense, Mom. It does seem that Duke would have a course that would give you answers like that."

Holy cow! What then am I doing in New York? There are no answers. And, the answer to the question of why did God let 6,000 innocent people die in the World Trade Center? That depends totally on personal theology.

Shall we ask, "Why did God let that woman's husband have an affair with his secretary? Why did God let the brakes on the car go out so that the teenager was killed in the accident? Why did God let the house burn down when the iron was left on? Why did the child fall out of a tree and break a leg? Why did God make the light turn red just as I was ready to go through it???" What about Lazarus? Yes, he was raised from the dead, but where is he now? Dead. So why did God let Lazarus die twice? The answers really start with your definition of God, the free will of humanity, and the natural laws of the universe. It seems to me that the best I can do is live by my own theology and then hope that it shows.

In Chinatown, on my last trip, I spoke to a young Japanese woman whose parents were atheists in Japan and they had brought up their children to believe that any form of religion was a cult and a type of brainwashing. She has been in California for a year, has just moved to NY, and has been studying all of the religions.

She finds it so confusing. She said, in her very broken English, "Every single religion says it is the only RIGHT way to believe. I don't know how that can be? I have roommates that are Buddhist and Muslim and Sikh and Hindu and Catholic. [She lives in a boarding house for foreign students.] They each believe with all of their heart that what they believe is right. How do I know?"

Obviously, I was absent the day they gave the RIGHT answer to that question. We spent well over an hour together; I felt as though I were trying to sell a product . . . Christianity, and my competition was stiff and committed. Was I, too, trying to brainwash her? The answer MUST lie in understanding our similarities and not focusing on our differences.

I was trying to get a cab on 50th Street West. It was after 10:30 p.m., not at all late by NY standards. Even the bars stay open until four a.m. on the weekends—the noise outside of my window affirms that. But it was 10:30 p.m. and there was a woman on the other side of the street who was trying to get a cab also.

Finally a cab pulled up to me, simply because he was in the lane closest to me. As I started to get in I could see that she was frantically waving to me across traffic, asking if she could share my cab. Of course, but be careful crossing through the traffic (once a mother—always a mother). She was about my age and size, but Hispanic. As we climbed into the back seat she thanked me profusely and said she was trying to catch a bus at a stop on Madison and 51st. (I was so excited that I knew exactly where that was. I had an earlier appointment on Madison and 55th.)

She shared that she was working late because she wouldn't be in the office again for two weeks and her husband in the Bronx would kill her (figure of speech) if she didn't catch this bus home. She is a corporate accountant. When she found out why I was in NY, she couldn't stop thanking me. But then she asked if I were a pastor. When I said yes, she started to cry. She has colon cancer (I didn't have time to recommend my detox center) and has to have another colonoscopy on Monday. Her husband will take her on vacation after that, to spend some quality time together away from her office. She asked me to pray for her and for her husband who is so worried about her.

As she prepared to jump out of the cab at her stop and was digging through her purse, I said, "Forget it I'll get the cab fare, you just make the bus." She hugged me and said I was her angel of mercy (she must be Catholic) and I wouldn't know how much she needed me that night. Then, poof, she was gone. I had done nothing . . . really . . . nothing. I certainly didn't have an answer for the question of why God has allowed her to have cancer. I must have been absent that day.

A Pastor's Journal
Entry Seventeen - NYC - Ground Zero
November 11, 2001

When I left the hotel at 6:55 a.m. I found the road blocked off and about thirty officers standing on the corner. In answer to my inquiry, the officers said that George W. Bush would go down this street today. He met at the United Nations today and spoke of the 86 countries that had lost citizens at the World Trade Center from the terrorist attack on September 11. Security is tight—extra undercover agents, extra police, and an extra challenge for NYC.

Bin Laden said today that he has nuclear and biological weapons, a statement that our government does not confirm or deny. What will be the end of this worldwide conflict? Here is part of a letter the bishops sent out this week:

> The message of the resurrection is that love is stronger than all the forces of evil. Furthermore, it is only sacrificial love, not war, which can reconcile people to God and to each other. We call upon the church, leaders, nations and individuals around the world to make room for love so that the patterns of our common life might reveal God's justice. We offer this letter with the wondrous promise of Advent ringing in our ears: "But the angel said to them, 'Do not be afraid; for see I am bringing to you good news of

great joy for all the people.'" (Luke 2:10) Peace,
The Bishops of The United Methodist Church

When I arrived at St. Paul's Chapel at the early hour of 7:20 a.m., I expected people greeting me to be impressed, or at least surprised. As many times as I hear that people are working at the site around the clock, it's easy for me to forget. I seem to get on with my own life and forget the immenseness of the damage of the terrorist attack.

At the crack of dawn it may as well have been the middle of the day. The sanctuary of St Paul's is now a shelter for workers. The bustle of activity included everything from serving breakfast to giving massages. Officers were taking naps on cots, reading cards from children all around the country, having their feet worked on, or picking up extra navy long-sleeve shirts because it was colder than they expected with the wind blowing. Yep, at 7:20 a.m. everything was in full swing.

At the front desk I was greeted and asked to sign in, write my SS# and the phone number of my next of kin. All of the volunteers must provide credentials, and the massage therapists, chiropractors, and podiatrists must bring copies of their licenses. (I guess they keep this information, both on premises and off.) They asked if I understood that St. Paul's was a possible target and under tight security since it is where all of the firefighters, police officers and iron workers come to be fed and for R&R. Sure, I knew it, but having to write it certainly made it more daunting. Good thing I had just read,

"Do not be afraid; . . . good news is for all people." I am not one bit afraid!!!

I met with the pastor of the church, a laid-back guy in his late thirties or early forties, I would say. We have a lot in common. Before September 11, his job was to start a Wall Street Gen-X Church. It met on Monday night. Of course he said, "Monday night, my congregation, if they are home by early Sunday morning church time, are still asleep." I concurred!) St. Paul's Chapel is under the auspices of Old Trinity church just a few hundred feet down the street.

Trinity Church History:

> There have been three Trinity Church buildings at Broadway and Wall Street. The present Trinity Church, designed by Richard Upjohn and consecrated in 1846, is considered a classic example of Gothic Revival architecture and is listed on the National Register of Historic Places. At that time, its soaring Neo-Gothic spire, surmounted by a gilded cross, dominated the skyline of lower Manhattan. Trinity was a welcoming beacon for ships sailing into New York Harbor.

> The Mayor of New York described the church as, "The glory of our City." The Parish of Trinity Church has played a pivotal role in the religious life of this city and our nation. Trinity Church has

started, endowed or aided more than 1,700 churches, schools, hospitals, and other institutions, and has always ministered to the needs of the poor and disadvantaged.

The city's first ministry to African Americans, both enslaved and free, began at Trinity in 1705. During the 19th and 20th centuries, Trinity offered special ministries to meet the needs and hopes of successive waves of immigrants who poured into New York.

The original burial ground at Trinity Church, which was used by all denominations, includes the graves and memorials of many historic figures, including Alexander Hamilton, William Bradford, Robert Fulton, and Albert Gallatin. The churchyard of St. Paul's Chapel, at Broadway and Fulton, also has many historic tombstones.

1696: Governor Benjamin Fletcher grants his approval for the Anglican community in Manhattan to purchase land for a new church.

May 6, 1697: Trinity receives its charter and a land grant from King William III of England. An annual rent of "one peppercorn" to the English crown is set.

1698:   The first building to house Trinity's worshipers was a modest rectangular structure with a gambrel roof and small porch. According to historical records, Captain Kidd lent his runner and tackle for hoisting the stones.

1705:   Queen Anne of England grants Trinity valuable acreage, increasing Trinity's holdings to 215 acres.

(. . . lots of history in between . . .)

1789: Following his inauguration at Federal Hall, George Washington attends thanksgiving service, presided over by Bishop Provost, at St. Paul's Chapel, a chapel of the Parish of Trinity Church. He continues to attend services there while the capital of the new republic is in New York City. St. Paul's Chapel is the oldest public building in continuous use in New York City.

So, today I sat in George Washington's booth and chatted with an officer while a podiatrist gave him injections in sore parts of his feet.

There was a tall distinguished looking man in a suit, tie and overcoat. I introduced myself to him.

He said, "Hey, I remember you . . . about a month ago outside."

How on earth??? He's with FBI and is a bomb specialist; he works with a black lab (he was dressed up because he was with the President's detail today). George Bush was to arrive here about one p.m. He said because of his job, he was very good at remembering faces and recalling situations. WOW!

As I write, I have already forgotten his name, but remember his dog's name. Maybe I will see him again. It was such a significant day to be at the World Trade Center. Not only was the date 11/11 . . . exactly two months after the terrorist attack on the WTC, but it was the day the President was arriving. It was the day that the United Nations was meeting and coming to view the WTC and to pay international respect to those who died there, but most importantly for me, it was Sunday.

The pastor graciously invited me to participate in the worship service, asking me to read the Epistle lesson to the Thessalonians. I don't think I have used the Book of Common Prayer since Divinity School (I'm ashamed to say), and most of the workers at the site are Catholic (although I found out NOT practicing, so they couldn't even tell the service wasn't Catholic!)

By far, most of the volunteers are Episcopalian, so the rest of the congregation was quite familiar with the BCP. The Pastor and his three assistants were in full clerics. The assistants were one woman, who is a priest and teaches homiletics at one of their Seminaries, an African-American Seminary Student, who is the Associate Pastor of St. Paul, and an Episcopalian

FBI Chaplain from Milwaukee. I was quite humbled. During the service of Eucharist, kneeling with wine and wafers, the sounds in the Chapel let us know that we were worshiping in the middle of the events set in motion on September 11. The workers came in and out as their break time permitted, and they were fed. Beepers went off and police scanners chattered frequently, cell phones and conversations were part of the service. Workers would participate a few minutes, cross themselves, and then go back out to the site. The subway would rumble underneath the floor and the shadows of a couple of flying birds could be seen through the opaque window behind the cross in the chancel area.

One high holy moment was the blessing of the cross that an ironworker had just brought in. It is a welded-steel cross from the rubble. It is only about eight inches tall and six inches wide, but what a symbol. After so long, we are still here and worshiping, in the shadow of the rugged steel cross—in a place where the history has been monumental, on land that has seen tremendous challenges in its 300+ year history—we are worshiping.

We are just passing through this brief life and I am just an instrument bearing the message that love is stronger than evil. Even the birds know it. They left for almost six weeks after the attack. Those pigeons that were a common sight around the financial district of NYC are back now and flew right behind the chancel during the service, one more strong symbol that life returns . . . shoot, I should have looked to see if one had an olive branch in its beak.

A Pastor's Journal
Entry Eighteen - NYC - Ground Zero
November 12, 2001

Mother Teresa said, "I don't look at the crowds, I look only at the individuals. If I looked at the crowds, I would never know where to start."

It is like that in New York. Today is Veteran's Day. Today with the crash of another airplane in New York, Belle Harbor is still grieving. This is a community that already lost over seventy of their neighbors who were firefighters at the WTC . . . and now this. They grabbed their garden hoses and tried to fight back. The neighborhood is devastated and the crowds, in pain, are growing before my very eyes. Two hundred and sixty people on the plane, all killed, plus eight on the ground not yet found, a whole neighborhood on fire, businesses exploded. A community is once again terrorized, but by terrorists? Perhaps not, we pray not, yet the fear is rampant.

I was concerned about the firefighters and police officers who had been working such long hours at Ground Zero. They had a holiday today. The site was closed down. They were so excited to spend some time at home . . . then this morning, at 9:25, they were called away from their Veteran's Day holiday to deal with the flaming wreckage in Queens. They are tired, emotionally exhausted.

Today I met three Federal INS agents—one from Texas, one from Kentucky and one from California—three different ethnic minorities. They are here for sixty days to find and apprehend illegal immigrants who might be connected with the terrorist attack. They are experts and can often tell, by observing, if someone is not who he is pretending to be. I like them and am proud they are working for me. We chatted about how their families are coping and what it's like to live in New York. (At least they each have small apartments in midtown.) We exchanged cards and they asked for prayer. We held hands and prayed together. I won't forget them—three individuals in a crowd of thirteen million.

I also met two 35-year-old partners who are too young to have to deal with their responsibilities at Staten Island. Evidently, the big scoops of debris at the WTC site are separated according to their origin; scoops from buildings one though five are kept as separate as possible. Then the separated remains go to Staten Island, where these two officers and all the others work twelve-hour shifts, around the clock, in complete HAZMAT uniforms. The debris is spread onto a grid like a football field and it is painstakingly raked for any remains that might be large enough to be raked out. Then it goes onto a conveyor belt that shakes everything into different sizes through sieves, and finally all the separated and sized material is examined meticulously. Even a tooth, which can mean a positive identification of one of the almost 6,000 dead, is treated with respect and returned as cremains.

At this point, nearly all families have provided DNA samples to the authorities. The officers fear that the process will take years. I ask how they can cope with it. They share that at first it was surreal, awful, and unbearable, but now they are used to it. "It's just our job. Hey, 3,000 officers quit, the first week, after 9/11. They couldn't take it . . . especially the rookies." It doesn't seem to me that these young men should have to be used to it. I must not look at the crowds.

A petite, 38-year-old, blond woman is a sergeant. She has three stripes on her left arm as well. I learn that each stripe signifies five years—she has been in the police department for fifteen years. Every police officer I talk with (almost 100 in all) measures his/her career in years until retirement. Twenty years . . . that's it. They all agree, "You just can't take it longer than that."

The morale of NYPD is low as a result of the current rocketing levels of stress. It's understandable that they are upset to make "half the pay of those on Long Island." The "honeymoon" is passing quickly and people are beginning to see the police not as heroes, but as "cops" once again. On the streets, the police are once again stopping some law-breaking citizens from doing what they want, and giving them tickets.

Two officers said that when they came out to get in their car yesterday, someone had spit on it and stuck chewing gum to the window. He gave me a big smile and said, "Hey, I thought we were the heroes of NY! You don't spit on a hero!"

Many of the officers affirmed the low self-esteem that comes from the taunting and negative reactions of the public. We talked a lot about handling feelings and remembering that what the public yells at them only reflects on the speaker not on the one being spoken to. We talked about letting go.

One set of officers wears special light blue coats. They go in and try to ease the tension in situations before having to make arrests. The younger guys are hot heads and don't have the wisdom to deal with people as well. (All the while I am carrying on some serious conversations with people, there is beautiful music playing in the background. Sometimes someone is playing the piano, sometimes a flute, sometimes a mandolin, but all peaceful . . . the language of the soul.)

A middle-aged woman in a red jacket from the American Red Cross grabs my arm and is quietly sobbing, "I'm sorry, I'm sorry, I just can't take it any more. How many more parts of bodies are they going to parade by our tent in there before it is finished? I just can't take it any more."

We talk, she cries. I listen, she cries. I get her a cup of hot chocolate with three fat marshmallows, we talk and finally she says, "I'm sorry I cried. I feel fine. I've got to run, I'm still on duty."

I have been making referrals to a personal trainer all day. Trying to talk officers and firefighters into going over to the table and letting the therapist stretch them. Oftentimes I go with them. It's bizarre for me to help them take off their things— bullet-proof vests, mace, Billy clubs, handcuffs, guns. I try not to look closely . . . all of those things remind me of violence and are frightening. However, the people who carry and wear them don't frighten me; I love the people I am dealing with. The same was true when, as a chaplain at Baptist Hospital in surgery, I thought I would faint every time I first entered an operating room and faced the smells, the instruments, and the austere atmosphere of surgery. However, when my patients finally came in and I could touch them, I was no longer overwhelmed. All people are just people when we get close to them.

I took my sandwich into a pew and sat beside the personal trainer. It wasn't more than two seconds before I had to give her my napkin because she was crying. She said it was the first time she had cried since she started working at St. Paul's. She wiped her tears and added, "What I do is so very little compared with what they do . . . I just don't know how they stand it."

Workers and volunteers alike feel that way. I would try to get the ironworkers to go get a free massage and they would say, "Give it to someone who needs it more than I do." We could all use a few lessons in grace and understanding that we are worthy because God created us and loves us exactly like we are. We don't have to outdo anyone else to be worthy for someone to care about us. We are worthy just as we are.

A man in a pew wasn't wearing a police uniform or a firefighter's uniform and didn't look ruddy enough to be one of the steel workers. I almost didn't speak . . . it felt a little out of the ordinary. It was. He is a doctor from Hawaii and is here to work for three weeks in the medical tent outside, in the "pit." So far he has just taken out metal splinters, bandaged ugly scrapes, and taken care of a few minor burns, but when we began to share stories, I told him that he was in ministry just as I am. He agreed. He said, "The WTC 'PIT' is a huge ugly sore and all of the workers and volunteers are white cells rushing to it to heal it." Great analogy!

He shared how touched he was with his very first patient. The construction worker had come over to St Paul's this morning to get a new pair of gloves (they go through them so quickly). He had picked up the work gloves and, putting his hand down inside, he had felt a piece of paper. Taking it out, he read aloud the words of a child's handwriting, "We are proud of you and want you to wear these new gloves to keep your hands warm. We will think of you. You think of us. Signed, Boy Scout Troop # ..." Well, at that point, the doctor and I both were wet with tears, but he wasn't finished with the story. He said, "The construction worker held up his badge. It was also # ..."

This is truly the ministry of presence. Be where they are, hear what they want to tell you, and love them, period. The hardest part of the day for me was when a group of eight army guys came in wearing camouflage fatigues. Being an Air-Force brat, I am attracted to men in uniforms (Deborah!!!). At first it was "May I get you anything?" They ate, they drank, and they walked around and were obviously choked-up as they read hundreds of letters. They took pictures and nobody stopped them. Then I sat down with three of them, aged 25, 26, and 32. They wanted to talk. It seems they are the next to be deployed to Afghanistan out of Ft. Bragg, in Fayetteville. It breaks my heart. Their six-month training had been condensed into one month, with generals doing lots of briefing, and their submitting to lots of testing. They are smart as whips and are ready to go, but I must have touched the mother-son strings in them, because soon we were hugging and tearing and they ask for my card. (So Rachel, Tyson, Julie and Cris, if they are at Ft. Bragg, over Thanksgiving, we will have three more at our table . . . you know we always have room for more!)

There must be a better way to solve our differences than war. I don't want those young men to have to experience war. I hate what they would have to do and see. It will take me longer to pray now. Camille, you must not look at crowds, only individuals. I have heard that whatever you pray for, YOU SHOULD BE. I promise, I will try.

A Pastor's Journal
Entry Nineteen - NYC - Ground Zero
November 13, 2001

We all need support. I'm just one beggar helping another beggar find food—no magic here. My heart touches theirs and we struggle together. Then we just get through each day the best we can. Today is better; my "suitemate" is gone. He must have been here just for the long weekend because no one is next door now—no slamming of doors, no smoke sneaking under the door; except for the street noises . . . it's quiet. My gosh, I feel like I'm in a palace . . . no one with whom to share the 'facilities' for a few days; I hope!

I was the only Ground-Zero Methodist Chaplain over the weekend. It seems UMCOR pulled out on Friday and turned the operation over to the NY United Methodist Conference. I was so busy, I didn't even notice that no one else was here. It's going to be difficult for the New York Conference to get a program going to take care of this enormous disaster. I remember all of the challenges we had in NC after the flood . . . this one is mind-boggling. It will certainly take a while for it to become a well-oiled machine.

After the plane crash on Monday, it took all day to get the organization in place, but by nine p.m. ten chaplains had arrived; seven were Native Americans from the Oklahoma/Texas Indian Conference, two were ordained, and five were laity. New York had specifically asked for Native Americans to work with the large population of Native

American steel workers. It's a joy to be able to work side by side with these Methodists. While the two of the clergy were riding in a cab, the woman pastor asked the driver what kind of music he was playing, commenting that she said she had never heard anything like it before.

He said the music was Dominican. She paused a moment then said, "I guess you are pretty sad about the plane that went down yesterday in Queens."

His mood grew very somber and he replied, "Yes, my cousin was on that plane."

Ministry is everywhere. In her first few hours, the Native American pastor from Oklahoma had an opportunity to minister to a fellow human in pain . . . far outside of her experience, yet joined in human need. Once again, God's call on each life comes at the intersection of human ability and human need. We are all one in Spirit.

Working in St. Paul's again, I am awed by its holy ground. Banners from all over the country, with hand written messages, hang from the balcony. The balcony is being used as storage for literally tons of supplies, non-perishable food, extra gloves, shoes, and whatever. In each pew, letters are taped about so that no matter where a rescue worker sits, there are words of encouragement and love in full view. Clean pillows, with donated angel pillowcases, and freshly folded blankets are pilled up at the ends of each pew, waiting for those workers who are blessed with precious periods of forty winks. One officer was waking another, teasing him about how loudly he was snoring. The awakened one countered, "It's just the music from the violin that put me to sleep." We all laughed. His partner said, "The music just started . . . you've been shaking the rafters for ten minutes." Ha ha.

I was standing by the coffee table when around the corner walked the middle-aged Red Cross woman from yesterday; the one to whom I gave the hot chocolate with big marshmallows. She had on her red vest and a hard hat. In her hand, not in her pocket, but in her hand, she held a card. She put her arms around me and placed the card in my hand.

"This is for you," she said. "It's an Angel-In-Your-Pocket card. Yesterday, you were my angel. I'm fine today, thanks."
I could hardly speak; there was such a lump in my throat.

That reminds me; one day when Tyson was about six he came home and looked a little sheepish. "What's wrong?" I asked.

"Well," he hemmed and hawed. "Do you know how hard it is to talk to the principal with a lump in your throat?" So cute, however, as the years went by . . . he got better at it. Ha ha.

It troubles me that I don't even know that Red Cross worker's name. Actually, our interaction yesterday was quite brief—it must have been the big fat marshmallows on the hot chocolate.

There are 44,000 police officers in the City of New York. It's not surprising that they don't know each other; they have been pulled from their own precincts in the far corners of the city to work here at the World Trade Center Site. I have the opportunity to know more of them each day. It's great to recognize some of them as they come in on their breaks. Today two, whom I had talked to yesterday, said they would have to take me out for real pizza. "Midtown doesn't have ANY REAL pizza." They are adorable and such authentic people. They had to tell me they are Italian—I'm so embarrassed to not be able to see the differences and tell one ethnic background from another. I don't notice unless they tell me.

There were two construction workers sitting by themselves, not in the pews but on the unoccupied massage tables, eating. I went over to eat with them. Their English was quite broken and they beamed with pride as I asked questions about their part in the project. They operate the gigantic claw-like things, grabbers I think they called them, which pick up the mammoth steel beams and put them in the trucks.

The number of truckloads recovered in any one day depends on how many times in a twelve-hour shift they have to stop work for special recovery operations, when a body is found. The entire site closes down in a show of respect until the body is removed on a Gurney and taken into T-MORT, the temporary mortuary or morgue. The two mechanical-claw operators used their hands to describe the procedure, to explain the throttles and levers. You would have thought that I would have to drive one tomorrow—their pride is evident. They skipped through or over some parts of their descriptions, as if thinking, "Oh, she'll never understand this."

They were so very dirty. I told them how worried I am for the health of their lungs. Do they always wear their HAZMAT re-circulating masks? Oh no. This work is so dangerous that the entire cab on their crane (or whatever it's called) is sealed and has tanks of air to circulate fresh air through it at all times. I asked them if I could get them more to eat or drink. They said no but each embarrassedly opened his pocket to show me another sandwich. They wouldn't get another break for a long time. I told them they could fill their pockets. I could tell they would not have taken the liberty to hug me, thinking I wouldn't have wanted to hug them, as dirty as they were. Even when I put out my hand, they expressed their feeling of being too dirty to shake my hand. I took their hands. Too dirty? No way, I shake hundreds of hands . . . we share the dirt. I'm proud to have your dirt on my hands; we're all in this together.

"I'm six-foot-two and weigh 225 pounds," the sergeant said. "Nobody messes with me. I can turn over a desk with one hand and back off a bunch of wild drunks with a stare."

We talked a long time, much longer than his break, I'm sure. He answered his scanner often. (Hmm, I thought scanners are only one way . . . wonder what he is talking into???) Before long we were talking about his handicapped child. He would, no, could retire in three years but needed good schools for his child with special needs. He was softening.

It wasn't long before he was retelling stories from his long career, stories of events which had affected him deeply. He talked about a father who had killed his infant for crying and how hard it was for him not to just "take out" the father, himself. Instead he had called his wife and asked her to go right then and kiss their baby. He openly cried as he shared about the beautiful woman in her thirties, with the debilitating illness, who had drowned herself.

He told of the difficulty he had reading the note that began, "Dear Officer, if you are reading this, I am dead and I am so sorry you have to be the one to find me. Please call my dad . . .." She had worn a bathing suit . . . modest even in death. He said he just "lost it" at her funeral. We went through all of those details and those of the death of one of his partners. He kept saying, "We must stop talking, this is so upsetting," but he couldn't stop talking. At last, I asked if these memories were so vivid because of the World Trade Center event. He thought and said, "I guess so, and I've never before talked about them or even remembered all of the details before. I had three of my own men killed in the building." (Oh, by the way . . . he had failed to mention that little detail.) "Thanks, thanks for listening. I've got to get back out on the street; my men will be wondering where I am." So, all six-foot-two, 225 pounds of him got up, hugged me, smiled, and said, "See ya later."

I understand "tandem jump" is a term used in skydiving. It's done with a novice attached to a jumpmaster, someone who teaches and has jumped many times before. The novice is harnessed to the front of the master and just goes along for the ride, in the safety of past experience. It's like that, I think, with people. Sometimes, no matter how proficient we may be at other things, we just don't know how to jump by ourselves. Maybe I just let them be harnessed to me for a few minutes, since I know what it feels like to be in pain, anguish, sorrow, despair, and grief. I know from experience that one can survive and even sometimes thrive in the face of such challenges. Maybe that's all I can do, be here to ride with them until they feel safe again.

A Pastor's Journal
Entry Twenty - NYC - Ground Zero
November 14, 2001

The Director of Pastoral Care for the New York Conference asked me to be in charge of the first debriefing meeting for the chaplains here this week, since he would be unavailable. We started at 8:30.

It has been a month since I first came to Ground Zero and I had forgotten the sheer magnitude of the experience of visiting the site for the first time. I had the opportunity to experience that shock of seeing it for the first time AGAIN, through the eyes of the new chaplains. It was difficult for one young Native American woman who works a few blocks from the Oklahoma City Bombing Site because the devastation here brought back all of the Oklahoma pain and horror.

The wall of memories, all of the flowers, candles, letters, banners, pictures—these are heartbreaking for all who see the scene, but for her it has the added impact of the heartbreaking memories of those lost in her own state. Even though it has been six-and-a-half years, people still light candles and leave memorabilia at the memorial wall.

Another young woman said she just couldn't talk, that if she tried she would "lose it" and wasn't ready to do that with us. I understood. They all talked of the horrible smell and the thickness of the air from the debris. It made me wonder if I had become immune after such a short time to the "war zone."

I didn't notice the horrible smell or those walking down the streets in masks, nor even the Martian-looking HAZMAT masks which are so commonplace. With them, I saw it all again; it came back into focus. How could I not notice?

A young police officer, with whom I had spoken yesterday, came into St. John's today and gave me a NYPD cap. It wasn't until I got it home that I realized his name is inside. What a very special gift. One of the volunteers, with whom I had spent a brief time after the soldiers had left the other day, returned to the center and brought me a T-Shirt. After her shift was over that day she had gone to the fire station where the officers are raising money for the families of the 300+ firefighters killed in the line of duty in the WTC. She bought me one of the special navy-blue T-shirts the officers were selling.   On the back of the shirt, there is a scene of NY skyline.   However, where the twin towers used to stand now stand a fireman and a police officer, larger than life. Below the picture the caption reads, "THE OTHER TWIN TOWERS OF NEW YORK ON 9/11."

My mother is always doing nice things like that for people; she is so generous and giving but I never think to. I'm a terrible gift buyer and usually just don't do it at all. Why is that? These two, the volunteer and police officer, are so thoughtful . . . am I not?

A woman was sitting in one of the pews, a little stooped over, in work clothes and a work jacket, with a knit cap pulled down almost to her wire rimmed glasses. She was eating something from a small bowl. For a split second, from her body language, I thought she just might want to be left alone. I started not to intrude but sat down on the pew in front of her anyway. I turned sideways and said, "Hi, how ya doin?"

She gave the obligatory one-word response, "Good."

Maybe I should leave her alone. Actually, there was only one guy, so far, who really just wanted to be left alone, so I continued with my spiel, "I'm Camille and I'm a Chaplain from North Carolina."

"My dad grew up in Virginia."

Life, maybe? "Really? I graduated from high school in Virginia."

"He did too!" The ice broke between us. She straightened up. Wow! She is tall, lanky, and young! Five minutes into the conversation, she took off her hat. A couple of minutes later she released her hair from a ponytail and a waterfall of beautiful long blond hair spilled out. Clark Kent changes into Superman and an inconspicuous, reserved stranger evolves into a Wonder Woman!

She has three (or four) college degrees and is currently a Conservator supervising the work on the tombstones between St. Paul's and Trinity that were damaged by the WTC disaster. In animated conversation, she explained the process of restoring the 300-year-old stones.

It seems that the debris (we affirmed also mixed with human remains) was propelled with such force that it jammed particles of cement, gypsum and glass against the old stones, in some cases, completely filling the sculpted words with solid material and filling any cracks.

If the material filling the carving and crevices in the stone were to get wet, it could solidify again and expand to eventually destroy the tombstones. These stones are an important part of American history . . . and their preservation and restoration must be handled with kid gloves, literally. I had never even thought about the tombstones, one more facet in the unbelievably complex and widespread mass of destruction.

I was amazed by her transformation and animation when describing the preservation process, obviously her love. She is brilliant and beautiful. She told me about her family, about teaching at the University here in NY, about being an English major and doing a lot of writing for archeological journals. I was blown away by her knowledge and enthusiasm. We chatted and enjoyed each other's company for a long time, probably much longer than she meant for us to.

For some reason, at one point, I said, "You know, it is my belief that this disaster will effect your generation, the Gen-X'ers, more than any other generation. After all, you have pretty much led a charmed life up to this point . . ."

She became very still and her face turned very somber and serious.

I innocently continued, "So, what do you think? How have you and your friends been coping here in New York?"

The dam burst and she shared her story. She was married on September 14, 2001, only three days after, and in the same city as the attack . . . O my gosh! My heart ached for her as she told of the wedding, perfect in its planning for almost a year, to be held at the University. No one could arrive by plane, some drove from very far away . . . they considered canceling . . . how could they? Then she described the reception which couldn't be held at the Pier, on the Hudson River, as planned.

I asked, "Why not?"

"The Pier is was used as the temporary morgue." Oh, my God. Oh, my God! We both sobbed and had to share her breakfast napkin.

She had long finished eating the scrambled eggs in her small bowl. We shared the details of the wedding that was supposed to be . . . then the details of the wedding that came to be. We even laughed together (often) about how hard we were crying together. We talked of the unfairness of it all and the anger, the frustration and, yes, even the joy. We talked much about life in the midst of death and the power of the moment. We shared thoughts about the importance of, and need for, an intimate relationship at a time such as this and then we cried even harder. (She was unaware that some of my tears were due to the fact that my own life is without an intimate relationship.) We discussed reevaluating the demands of her current job and the possibilities for spending more quality time with her new husband. We really bonded. What a precious gift she is to me . . . and to think that, for a split-second, I considered not reaching out to her. Thank you, God!

There are now 600 Red-Cross trained and certified chaplains working at the WTC site and also at the crash site of the airplane that took off from New York on its way to Santa Domingo yesterday, where 260 passengers perished. Out of those 600 chaplains, I was only the seventh United Methodist to be certified. It was supposed to be a two-hour training session, but it took six hours. I hated having to give up my time at St. Paul's to do it. I took the train from the Financial District to St. John, the Divine Cathedral, a gorgeous place that I had never been before. It is near Union Theological Seminary, just a couple of blocks from the General Board of Global Ministries for the UMC. Both inside and out, St. John looks like Notre Dame de Paris, in France, but maybe bigger! Our training was in another building however. They are desperate for chaplains, especially after the crash yesterday.

Once again, it amazes me how life experiences build on one another. In 1976-77 I had been the Director of Volunteers for the American Red Cross in Durham. The training was therefore quite familiar. Afterwards, we walked just a couple of blocks to the train, rode downtown for fifty-some-odd blocks, changed trains and rode south, going under the bay, all the way to Brooklyn, where Red Cross has its headquarters. We waited in line to make copies of our new certificates; then we waited in line to exchange copies of our credentials, certificates, ID's and driver's licenses, for legal documentation (if only the terrorists had to go through this much red tape!) We waited in another line in another room to have our ID pictures taken; then we waited in line on another floor to pick up our hard hats, masks, safety goggles, and Official Red Cross Chaplain Vests.

When it was all finally done, we rode the train back from Brooklyn to Midtown. It was quite an exhausting ordeal, especially after my having already worked six hours at St. Paul's.

At the group meeting, there were some who expressed feelings of affirmation after having been certified by Red Cross. (It is a rather impressive procedure!) Then there were some who expressed negative feelings about not having the necessary credentials to be certified by Red Cross, and feelings of maybe not being valuable and of perhaps wasting their time volunteering. I shared my thoughts with the group that having degrees behind one's name means only that one knows how to pass tests. I assured them that, for more than three weeks, I have done plenty of ministry work here at the WTC site, without the stamp of approval from the Red Cross, and there is an overwhelming amount of ministry here; everyone is greatly needed. Ministry comes from one's heart and it is WHO WE ARE at the very core of our being . . . after all, our true authority is not from the American Red Cross; it's from God.

A Pastor's Journal
Entry Twenty-One - NYC - Ground Zero
November 15, 2001

A young man boarded the subway car and sat by me. At first glance, I saw that his skin was covered in tattoos of all different colors. At second glance, I noted that he had many skin piercing sites on his body. I had no personal contact with him but the woman sitting at his other side asked him about the skin piercing and I overheard their conversation. He said he has twenty-three piercings and nineteen tattoos. He had his blond dreadlocks held back from of his face by a red headband and was wearing inch-round earrings that were framed by inch-round holes in his ears. In his words, it's his art form.

He took out one of his earrings to demonstrate and a woman sitting directly across from him began gagging. She covered her ashen face and turned sideways in her seat. The woman beside him was about my age and didn't sound judgmental as she asked more about the pain, desire, and opinion of his peers, etc.

I was interested in learning also, so didn't hide my own curiosity. He told us that he's engaged and showed us his ring. He and his fiancé had both chosen the same ring. I assume that hers, like his, is stapled through the ring finger of the left hand, coming out on the underside. I, too, experienced that gagging sensation.

We all then rode in silence until a dirty and tattered homeless man, mentally handicapped and loud, entered the far end of the car. Everyone looked disgusted. There were lowered heads, slow blinking eyes, and slight shakes of the head, as if to say oh no, not this again.

He asked for money, "Just for food." Yeah, right, more shakes of the head from most passengers. He ambled down the full length of the car asking everyone, as he swayed with the car's side-to-side motion, but no one budged, not one penny . . . that is until he got to where I was sitting. Without hesitation, the dreadlocked, tattooed, and pierced young man reached in his pocket and took out a dollar for the beggar. I couldn't help but feel guilty for all of my fears, my shallowness, and even for my sheltered life of plenty. Oh, the lessons I have still to learn in God's wide world.

I was blessed to make my first trip into the pit with an Episcopal priest who is also a retired history professor. I was fortunate to have my hard hat in hand when he asked if I would like to walk the site. In full garb, yellow hard hat and chaplain vest, we took the two-hour walk.

The Red Cross credentials will get me everywhere the President of the United States can go, probably further, because he can't be exposed to any danger. There had been a sprinkling of rain so the dust wasn't so bad. Fire hoses gush large plumes of water at all times in the actual digging site to keep the fires and dust down.

It had been drilled into me that this is a federal crime scene and nothing is to be disturbed or removed but, to me, it is much more. Upon this ground thousands of human bodies have been disintegrated. In the blink of an evil eye, what had happened where I stood changed millions of lives forever. This crime scene is holy ground.

The priest spoke of when each of the collapsed buildings had been built, of how tall each was and of what type construction. With each turn, he would look at the remaining skyline and tell me of the history of a powerful financial district, the most powerful in the world. The first wave of fear I had, since arriving, came when we walked under one of the buildings that was only half blown away; yes, it was supported by steel beams but the gaping wound was close enough to touch. I was struck by a brief moment of panic; at any moment, this building might collapse on me! The panic passed.

I am sorry that some of his very valuable data fell on deaf ears because I was totally absorbed by what my eyes were seeing. I could see papers on the desks and a sweater hung on the back of a chair, covered with gray dust and debris, as if frozen for eternity. I felt as if I were in the twilight zone. As he talked, I kept trying hard to swallow the lump stuck in my throat.

There were filing drawers open and filing drawers closed. There were eight by ten-inch photographs still standing on bookcases with books still on the shelves; what looked like a pocketbook was hanging on the back of a chair. But everything was gray, as if we were looking through a veil. It was as if a gust of wind had suddenly come down the chimney, blowing a winter's worth of soot and gray ash all over everything. There were no walls to block our view; the moment in history was frozen right there, out in plain view. For an instant, I thought the office workers should be allowed to get those things out of their rooms and desks, but then I remembered the danger. No one can safely go in there.

We visited the temporary morgue where a chaplain is on duty, 24 x 7, paying respect and offering prayers for the dead, as the newly discovered body parts are brought in. A man I had met during my training was on duty. He asked if I could come back and work in his place if his replacement didn't come soon. "Of course." I would have no problem working either in that morgue or the one for the plane crash, where they asked if I would work. However, my real call is to the living . . . dealing with normal (I use that term lightly), everyday survival issues. He said he would come to St. Paul's to get me if I were needed. He hasn't come and I am glad.

T-MORT is stark. If I were in charge, there would be calming music playing at all times; Generic, so as not to offend anyone, both classical and current, maybe Enya, soothing, renewing. I would have fresh flowers in the tent, so that even the stark stainless-steel Gurneys would seem more like furniture . . . flowers for a welcome home, a coming home; after all, that's exactly what it is. There is nothing to be afraid of in the morgue; graduation has taken place.   The spirit is gone and only the physical home remains, whether parts or the whole . . . the spirit is already gone, no reason for fear here.

I saw many young police officers in the pit and they would nod as if we were comrades in this together. But then I would touch their respirator masks hanging around their necks and say, "Officer, put this on . . . the air quality is too bad for you to be without it."   They would complain about how uncomfortable it is and how the air isn't so bad today because the wind isn't blowing, ya da, ya da.   I would simply say, "Officer, the appropriate answer is, 'Yes, Mother.'"   They would each smile and nod. The young never have the foresight to see what can happen to them 20 years down the road.

The OSHA people who come into St. Paul's talk about all of the poisonous gases coming from the pile. They tell of how they've done over 20,000 air samples and how they try to explain to the workers that the respirators (HAZMAT masks with the two Martian-like round boxes on either side) are necessary. Evidently everyone digging by hand or with small machinery does wear a HAZMAT, but they all should. You can't assume that just because the debris is not blowing that the air is safe to breathe.

We walked by a small makeshift, three-sided plywood memorial to a certain group of union workers. They were the custodians of the different buildings.   Once again, seeing the candles, flowers, pictures, letters from children to their daddies, teddy bears, and banners, reminded me of those who don't receive the attention that the fallen firemen have.

I felt a little panic as we walked under a crosswalk that's still in place. It leads to the Marriott and is supported with beams. It is so very obvious why the site is off-limits; I have never, in my life, seen such large vehicles beeping as they are backing up. The massive pieces of equipment lift tons of cement structures at a time, with the grapplers (not grabbers like I heard of the other day.)

I am so concerned for the workers having to work twelve-hour shifts, seven days a week, every day, for seven weeks. I'm not sure the human psyche can take it. I have concern for their safety but even more concern for their mental and emotional health.

In the medical tent, a man was being treated for a glass wound in his leg. The chunk of glass had simply fallen from several stories up and ripped through his pants. We talked while the doctor from California stitched him up and the nurse from Florida (a firefighter herself) assisted. The wounded man said he knows how lucky he is not to have lost his leg.

My pants were muddy; my shoes were muddy and had to be washed off before we could enter the respite care center at St. John's University, "on the inside." There I chatted with three construction workers who were discouraged about having to take down the building; they are used to building, not tearing down.

They and their fellow union workers will probably be the ones to rebuild on this site . . . no telling how many years until that happens. The Jewish community opposes that ever happening; they believe nothing should be built on the "hallowed ground of a graveyard." Later that night I saw the same three men having dinner at St. Paul's. They kissed me on the cheek and we hugged as long-lost friends, so excited to see each other. It really is one more example of how very important community is, and relationship is, at a time such as this for our country. Pain and sadness are rampant everywhere I look.

Back outside, the priest and I worked our way through the "war zone." I saw an erected cross. As we got closer I noticed the rough edges and bent steel. "It is natural." My guide explained that it's a girder that was ripped from its position in one of the WTC buildings and fell to the ground, with the cross bar just where it is. It may be fifty feet tall. The rescue workers erected it on the pile and someone has a fifteen-minute service there each Sunday. They have no time off to go to their own churches. There is a huge American flag on the building behind the cross.

I noted that it stands very tall, that rusted, bent, and twisted steel cross, in the midst of a wilderness of exhaustion, death, and destruction wrought by evil—a somber symbol of hope.

A Pastor's Journal
Entry Twenty-Two - NYC - Ground Zero
November 16, 2001

We teach best what we need to learn. For the past week, I have been trying to get the workers to take the time to get free chiropractic work, foot care, and massages. Most of them (men and women) won't go because they think that someone else deserves it more. I make it a point to go around several times each day and check on the other volunteers, to see how they are holding up and if there is anything I can do for them. Usually I start with the welcome desk, move to the supply table, then to beverages, the food service, on to chiropractic, podiatrist, and end up at the three stations in the far front corner of the church, where three therapists are set up for massages behind white curtains.

One morning, there was no one in the stations having a massage and we four just chatted a while. The three therapists shared their experiences and about how they had gotten more from volunteering than they had possibly given. We discussed the theological significance of giving AND receiving. It has been my experience that most massage therapists are very spiritual and want to talk about it when given the chance; these were no different. They study a lot about holistic health and complementary health care before becoming certified. These three were quite spiritual.

On that day they nailed ME. The young man from California had been volunteering on and off for a while because his parents are residents in the financial district. He started on me first. "You, Camille, have been working here a lot; have you had a massage, yet?"

"No, I haven't. You aren't here to serve me, but the site workers."

"Really?" he asked. "It looks like to me that YOU work with everyone in here not just the site workers. In fact, you come to debrief us several times a day. Why haven't you gotten a massage?"

(Ummm, it must be the same reason that it is hard to talk the site workers into coming over for a massage. I feel like someone else deserves it more than I do. My socks are dirty from walking around on the site.)

In his cute, cocky little California way, he implied that I don't practice what I preach and that I should get on the table. The other two chimed in with what they know about the body holding stories of pain and stress.

I have to admit, it was difficult, difficult to take off my credentials and my jacket, difficult to take off my shoes and difficult to climb on the table and it made me angry with myself. I was being so stupid, I get massages all the time in Raleigh . . . naked! So what was the big deal? In reflection, I can see there was safety in my position as CHAPLAIN. I felt more vulnerable from having my identity taken away than from taking off my clothes.

Lying on the table (not doing, just being) in the hands of a stranger raised anxieties that I didn't want to acknowledge . . . what if the priest saw me and thought I wasn't doing my job? (Yes, I will have worked nine Red Cross shifts in one week; so, Camille, when is enough . . . enough?) What if the Sisters, with their double first names, dressed in their full-length black habits, thought it was inappropriate for a female clergy to be lying on a table in their sanctuary? What if the workers with whom I had been talking saw me and thought, "Is she is hurting as much as we are?"

So . . . what if all of that were true? Oh my gosh, all of those thoughts just about getting a massage. I think it was Emerson who said, "What lies behind us and what lies before us are tiny matters compared to what lies within us." No, kidding. This is more than I wanted to think about!

I was on my back and he, at the end of the table, lifted and held my head and neck in his hands for a long time. As he gently cradled my head, all the feelings of apprehension, fear, anxiety, nervousness, shame and unworthiness vanished; I let go instantly, when I felt him praying for me. Our energies became one as he surrounded me with love and light. For the first time since I had been in New York I moved into a deep meditative state. Colors drifted through my mind's eye and I floated through the heavens, in and out of sleep and dreams. He knew that I knew . . . and I knew that he knew. Amazing. What a precious gift . . . once again, I almost missed it. Must concentrate more on the theology of receiving as well as giving. God comes in many forms when we allow and perceive.

Later in the day my massage therapist caught up with me and we sat in a pew together to talk. (It is so very powerful that Trinity Episcopal has opened its doors in the midst of this disaster . . . every pew is holy, every moment spent inside is holy; this is what a church is called to be . . . a sanctuary in the wilderness. John Street United Methodist is a few hundred yards away . . . I would be doing this ministry there if it had responded in this way.) He shared the story of a much older woman, (perhaps in her seventies or eighties) his massage therapist instructor, who was so very wise and spiritual and he talked of the need to reevaluate his whole life after September 11. It was hard to believe he is only 27, had formerly owned a surf shop (maybe that's another reason I was so hesitant, ha ha), and had completed his massage training after September 11. We talked of weaving massage into a spirit-filled life. He returns soon to California. I must add him to my prayer list.

God's timing in its infinite wisdom is always perfect. The Conservator, my Wonder Woman has taken a new job. "What is there not to like?" That was her husband's response when he heard about the new job. "Besides, . . . this . . . and that . . . means you and I will spend more time together." He joked, "hmmm maybe we should think about it a little more."

In the blink of an eye, she changed her life and she couldn't wait to tell me. It is so very true, just as we say in Igniting Ministries: You never know when your one interaction with someone will change a life. We had thrown our arms around each other at first meeting, and then I got to hear the news even before her parents. The powerful University job had been in the works for a while, but only yesterday had she decided to accept it. She wore a huge grin on her face and accompanied her narration with dramatic gestueres. She got a bowl of oatmeal and I listened intently to every detail of the new possibilities. The new job won't start for a month or two, so the tombstones were still on her mind. She took me through the back corridor of the church and out a gigantic 300-year-old two-ton door (well maybe not quite two tons) and into the cemetery.

Going straight to the tent, we wore our respirators. Inside the totally enclosed tent, the debris had been removed and the dirt had been meticulously removed to exactly two inches below the ground level. Even though it was solid black dirt, it was so level, packed, and clean that it looked like I could eat off of the floor. Perhaps it just seemed overly clean and tidy because it was such a drastic contrast to the destruction and devastation OUTSIDE of the tent. One of the men was carefully vacuuming the dirt particles from around the base of one headstone; in his garb, he looked like a Martian. There were probably ten to fifteen tombstones inside the tent and three or four coffin-shaped, but larger, above-ground markers.

I said, "Oh yeah, some people wanted to be buried above ground sarcophagus style." (Oh, was I ever thankful to remember that big word.)

She laughed, "OK, Camille, come check out the contents."

Since these were the tombs closest to the WTC collapse, this one had about a square foot of its side blown out and was to be repaired. We smiled together as I peered in . . . EMPTY no bones; nothing . . .oh well, limestone doesn't protect much does it?

We walked out into the graveyard and she told me historical facts, most of which went way over my head . . . a lot about the construction of St. Paul's and the types of materials needed to clean off all of the debris so as not to cause permanent damage.

We looked at inscriptions, very difficult to read with all of the debris blown into them, but possible using special lights and reflective mirror-type equipment. I reached into one of the crevasses to touch and rub the ash between my fingers, some of it gray and powdery, obviously composed of different materials. I didn't hear her next few sentences as I thought about the buildings that once stood so close, making the skyline so recognizable.

A cab driver told me that as he drives back and forth over the bridges each day, coming from home and taking people to and from the airport, he looks at Manhattan and it appears to be a body without a head. I thought of the metal and equipment on the airplanes, of the technology and computers; I thought of the creative genius of thousands of men and women blown to bits and now between my fingers; I thought of the thousands of innocent lives snuffed out in an instant; I thought of their brilliance, their potential. I rubbed part of them between my fingers. I thought of the tombstone I had just touched and what the ones newly buried here might have thought if they had known how important their contributions might have been to the history of the United States. I also, thought of those young terrorists, willing to die for their cause. I rubbed particles of them as well, between my fingers. "Jesus said, Father, forgive them for they know not what they do." That is not just true for huge disasters, but anytime love is not the motive. I must forgive. Why? Because not to forgive only hurts me and keeps ME from being an instrument of love and light.

This week, a man said he was trying to explain what happened to his five-year-old child without being too frightening, knowing that the story would come out anyway on TV or at school. He explained that bad men took over big airplanes and, on purpose, flew them into big buildings and lots of people died because of what they did.

The child thought for a minute and then said, "Daddy, they are going to have to say they are sorry, aren't they?"

It's too late for that; they can't and won't say they are sorry. However, I know that I must forgive them anyway . . . all of them. I drop the ashes back to the ground in the graveyard . . . sort of appropriate, I think, and then I say, "I forgive them." Then I ask God to forgive me, for really not wanting to forgive them.

A Pastor's Journal
Entry Twenty-Three - NYC - Ground Zero
November 17, 2001

The very young police officer looked half asleep. I said, "Hi, I'm Camille and I'm a Chaplain from North Carolina. Is there anything I can get for you?"

"Oh, my God, do I look that bad?"

"No, why?"

"Well, me and my buddies had a blow-out party last night, the first time since September 11. You know they've taken us out of our precinct and scattered us all over the place so we don't even see each other anymore. Honest, it is the first time we've had a party or anything. I was just in here trying to catch a few winks before I'm back on duty."

I laughed. "No, honey, you don't look THAT bad. I was just asking if I could get you anything, but you do look awfully guilty. There's no need to apologize to me!"

"Oh, good, then let me tell you about the party. Ya da, ya da. . ."

Two days later he came up to me and introduced me to two more very young police officers. "These guys were at my house for the party I was telling you about."

The four of us ended up talking through their whole break, probably longer. They spoke of stresses and strains and of being sick of their schedules and of being pulled off their regular detail to go to the plane crash. When I ask them how they were grieving, they blew it off.

"Grieving? We're so busy we hardly have time to live, never mind grieve . . ."

It will be harder down the road when all of these thousands of rescue workers DO have time to grieve.

"We have just gotten used to working our shifts down here . . . at least we rotate now. We deal with people coming by all day. Most of 'em are pretty nice and you can tell the out-a-towners, they're really nice to us, thank us for being here, and stuff, but we're just doing the job we have to do, it's not too bad."

They are upset about there being no time for any social life; I nod and say it's pretty frustrating. They fuss about the firefighters a while and then talk of the friend who had been in the building and died. They act as if it should be no big deal to them because he was just one friend and so many were killed. We talk for a little while about how many lives each person affects, how our feelings are important and how the magnitude of the impact on each of us doesn't depend on the number of those lost. None of these guys has a spiritual community. Briefly I wished I could live up here and start a church especially for all of these young people so directly affected by 9/11.

I did something I wish I hadn't done. St. Paul's is so fabulous and is doing such a wonderful ministry at Ground Zero. In addition to all the free services, volunteers and space they provide, (It really is a huge operation to run around the clock!) they have a Eucharist service at noon every day. The bell rings and three or four clergy in full dress walk down the center isle and hold a complete service of Holy Communion, straight from the Book of Common Prayer.

During the services, there are thirty to sixty workers and twelve to twenty volunteers in the back who do not participate. They continue eating and milling around while only two to five people take part in the service (that's right, two to five people). You can tell who is participating because they sit up front, knowing when to stand, sit, and provide all the appropriate responses. The brief homily is always appropriate and well executed, but the acoustics are poor and, with no P.A. system, I can't hear much from the back. The last time I was in St. Paul's during a service, I continued talking to some people in the back. It seemed such a perfect opportunity for relevant spiritual sharing with a captive audience.

I made the mistake of asking the priest, "Father, does it bother you that only a couple of people participate in your service when all of the workers are in here?"

"No," he replied. "It is just one more thing that we offer in addition to everything else, and whoever wants to participate may." He then walked away.

I was so angry with myself. Camille, why can't you just keep your mouth shut? This ministry is fabulous. Practice what you preach, for goodness sake. You always say it is fine no matter how others choose to worship. Here the Episcopalians have a different idea about worship and theirs is MUCH OLDER than yours. So shut up.

At home in Raleigh, I am happy to have started a faith community called Hope in the Wilderness. This mission segment, the reaching out to others in New York, is called "Voice in the Wilderness." I hope to start different missions later. The self-study segment—reaching into self—could be called "Journey in the Wilderness" and include personal growth, self understanding, mental and emotional health, growth groups, classes, and lectures (all of this is just brainstorming, so who knows?) The third segment should be for spiritual growth—reaching up to God—and could be called "Path in the Wilderness." I'm thinking that it would complement what churches offer.

Some who would want to participate would already have a church home while others may not have a church home and this could serve as their faith community. It should meet on a weeknight and be based on a scripture text with a relevant theme, and possibly be interactive in nature (like all of the new video games). People, placed around tables or in small groups, would have a chance to talk with their neighbors about how that particular topic affects them. Perhaps other sources are available that could provide references on the same topic. There is a need for faith communities such as these, especially among Gen X'ers.

Oh how I wish I could put hundreds of these people from Ground Zero in my pocket and somehow plug them into the Hope In the Wilderness community. They have such spiritual needs; they have only recently started telling me about them.

One man said, "I don't believe in priests."

"What about me?"

He said, "Well, I don't believe in preachers. I guess I don't believe in chaplains either." (But we had been talking for thirty minutes.) He then described his Catholic background and why he was on the path he was. However, he certainly wanted to keep talking about it.

Another shared about all of the different religions in his family. He told me about his "bottom line" to understanding all faiths and said that he couldn't understand what all of the disagreement was about.

One asked me, after three earlier conversations, "Who let you be a chaplain anyway? What does a chaplain do? Don't you have a real job?"

Oh my, the harvest is ripe. So many are ready to entirely re-evaluate their understanding of life, at least what they knew of it before 9/11.

I again saw the young man who has lost all of his friends from the 104th floor of WTC. He survived only because he had been on vacation and is now experiencing an extreme case of survivor's guilt. He was carrying a small shopping bag.

"What's in the bag?" I asked.

"An old shirt." I must have looked as though I was going to hit him with another question because he quickly added, "I spilled my lunch on the one I wore to work today and had to go buy a new one, to meet you tonight." Hmmm, he might be healing a little . . . he could have canceled.

He was wearing kaki pants and what looked to be a light blue Oxford- style dress shirt (probably silk or just as fine). His shirtsleeves were rolled up and he appeared quite yuppyish, especially with his new haircut. Yes, he got a haircut. Maybe he has passed through the worst. How long has it been now, eight weeks, nine? I can tell he is better; he fussed at me, about me, and about everyone else in his life for over an hour. He fussed about his parents and about how no one can understand what he is going through. He fussed about my journal and told me what I should write in my journal (I didn't act on his suggestions, but nodded as if I might). He has moved into the anger stage of grief . . . that's good.

Anger's not a bad thing when dealing with grief; in fact the relationship between anger and grief is similar to that between love and hatred. Hatred is NOT the opposite of love . . . NOT FEELING ANYTHING is the opposite of love . . . ambivalence is the lack of thought or lack of concern. Crimes of passion are committed out of a feeling of hate, usually for someone they have loved or for someone keeping them apart from one they love. Ambivalent people don't care about someone enough to even think about a crime . . . lack of thought is the opposite of love.

Here, not allowing yourself to feel anything can keep you from getting beyond depression, shock, and denial. Anger is appropriate and one of the stages of grief to follow shock and denial. He still has a long way to go and rightfully so; no one can imagine how he feels or what he is going through.

It is not God's will that this happened to him nor to the millions of people affected by the WTC attack. I can never know exactly how any of them feel. There are no appropriate platitudes; no statements such as, "You will feel better soon," "You are young and will get over this," or "Just be grateful you were on vacation and didn't get killed" can ever make this better. In truth he must walk his own path in his own way. I do say, "My heart aches for you. I cannot begin to imagine what you are going through. The country and my friends back home share your grief and care deeply about what you are experiencing. I pray for you daily." I also say, "What can I do to help you? I will do anything. Do you need for me to shop for the things on the list we made last week?" "No," is still his reply. I do feel that he is a little better though; the tears do not flow with each sentence. He is now angry and I'm glad for him.

I must be sure to not put too much importance on the time I spend with this young man. I must keep reminding myself that I can't make him better. That is his work to do. Trying to do all of the work in any relationship is not loving . . . it is sick. Being the one to always fix and always care is destructive and not healing. I have been in relationships in which I always had to be the one giving. Some people are used to being bailed out of their dilemmas: financial, emotional, and professional. However, balance in any relationship is of paramount importance. To give too much is to enable the other person to be irresponsible for the relationship and for himself. To give too much is to give of one's own sickness and need. To give too much is not ministry; it's self-indulgence.   Balance is everything.

Even with my children, I am not always the giver. I allow them to be givers also. I do not take care of anything in their lives that would keep them from taking care of it themselves. I will not be their crutch; how unfair of me that would be to them. Yes, they fuss, telling me how other parents pay some expense or bail their children out of a problem situation. In requiring them to solve their problems, I know I am helping them to be fully competent to take care of themselves as part of the next generation.

They tease me, saying that I would now never let them live at home. It is true, and they likely wouldn't want to. "You use hot water; you pay for it. You want heat to be warm; you pay for it or be cold. You want a nice car; get a better job."

Far too many of the current generation of youths fail to understand the logical consequences of their behavior. The logical consequence of my eating fattening foods is that I get fat. The logical consequence of not having a job (if I'm capable) is not eating. As a caring listener and pastoral counselor, it's important that I remember to not give too much. Some come to me for help but want to stay in the same mess that they are in. They want me just to tell them how pitiful their lives are and to feel sorry for them. I don't. It's just as important for my balance and me, as it is for them, to let them do their own work. We all have to meet our own responsibilities.

Healing just takes as long as it takes. As the doctor from Hawaii said, there is a gaping wound in our country. Sure, antibiotics will help a wound, but in the long run, it is the body itself that must do the mending and the healing. I'm sort of like an antibiotic, helping keep the infection in check so the body can heal itself. In the end . . .we can only heal ourselves. Thank goodness, humanity has a resilient spirit. We will heal, unless we get hung up thinking that our lot in life is less fair than anyone else's, unless we lie to ourselves about why we are in such a predicament, or unless we begin to enjoy the role of victim. Hopelessness is not permanent unless we choose it. Tears are not forever. I have heard they are like rain; they loosen up our soil so we can grow in a different direction. I pray that our country DOES grow in a different direction, because our soil has certainly been loosened with millions of tears.

A Pastor's Journal
Entry Twenty-Four - NYC - Ground Zero
November 18, 2001

I went by myself to Grand Central Station Oyster bar and ordered half dozen oysters on the half shell. My friends in Wilmington would croak if they knew that one half-dozen costs about the same as the half-bushels we used to buy and roast outside on the grill.

I had finished the oysters and was about to leave when a group of ten very happy and very friendly folks from the UK arrived. Their delightful British accents were pronounced. They asked if they could share my space while they waited for a table; they could see I was alone and they had so many people. I was immediately immersed in conversation, learning that they had arrived only a few hours before, that the oyster bar was their first stop, and that six of the ten had never been to the US before.

I asked, "Why now, of all times?"

They said, "To show we're NOT afraid of terrorists." They said it was also to show support for the New Yorkers and spend money and help the US economy. I later learned that while three wives had come with their husbands on this show-of-defiance trip, four other wives would not fly with their husbands.

I made the mistake of saying that I like Tony Blair and appreciated his speech the day after the terrorist attack. They agreed that his speech was OK but they don't like him. "He is such a COMMONER."

We certainly forget what a class system they have in the UK. It was obvious I was hobnobbing with the upper echelon! I expressed my gratitude, and I'm sure the gratitude of most everyone else here in United States, to the Queen for playing our National Anthem at Buckingham Palace for the first time in history.

They asked why I was in New York and alone. I shared that I would get on the train the next morning at seven a.m. and go down to the WTC site to work. They didn't asked what I do and it was no accident that I didn't offer to tell them. I was enjoying their company, they were having such a wonderful time, their language was so colorful, and they were giving me quite an insight into upper class England. It has been my experience that if I had told them that I am a Chaplain or even a preacher (for gosh sakes), I would have been totally shut out. I hate that part of being a pastor.

In 1981, the pastor of my home church in Durham, Aldersgate UMC wrote on my application for Duke Divinity School, "She will have a hard time separating herself from the sheep in order to be the shepherd." Even now, twenty years later, I still wonder if this is what he meant.

When their table was ready, we said our goodbyes. I wished them all a joyful stay as they headed toward the dining room. I paid my bill, stood up, and was putting on my coat when one of the English gentlemen returned from the dining room. He came up behind me and said, "My dear, we just took a vote and decided you should be part of our dinner tonight, so we've had the dear chap add another chair for you at the head of the table. Please grace us with your presence."

It was absolutely delightful; no, it was jolly good! I was wined and dined as a very special guest. It reminded me of the Igniting Ministry movie, "What if a special guest were going to come to your church next week; how would you treat them?" I have been in far too many churches where I did not feel the spirit of welcome. It would be nice if all churches were as kind to their strangers as these foreigners were to their stranger, me. It was such an honor to spend that time with them and hear all their stories and about how they travel around Europe together.

The men have been in a diners' club together for thirty years (no women allowed . . . do you permit that in the United States? Cute.) During the dinner, Rachel and Julie called me on my cell phone from a party in Durham. Each of my new friends at the table had to talk with them. Then, of course, I had to share part of my own story (but not the Chaplain part!)

Too soon, dinner was done. Before we separated, I gave them all of my train, bus and city maps, and offered blessings for a wonderful stay. We hugged one another and were each thankful for our serendipitous meeting.

My life is the one that has been blessed; but then I always am blessed. As usual, instead of me ministering to them, they ministered to me. My mother gets so upset that I'm never afraid, but why should I be afraid? Angels surround me and protect me. I am where God has called me to be, doing what God has called me to do. Therefore, whatever happens IS God's will. My dinner companions are one more example of God's grace shining in the moment, brightly and warmly . . . the right thing to happen in that moment.

At St. Paul's the next morning I met one of the ironworkers having his breakfast. He was ruddy, had a hint of red in his dirty blond hair and very light eyes . . . maybe blue or green but very light (being from a family of nothing but dark brown eyes, I always notice light eyes). He was wearing many layers of clothes (the temperature in church is kept fairly low so as not to overheat the workers who always have on so many clothes when they come in).

The ironworker's demeanor was coarse but he was very polite. It was so obvious that his life had not been so easy as mine had. As he prepared to go back to work, he thanked me for eating breakfast with him (but I didn't eat). I reached out to take his hand but he was reluctant to let me shake it. He said he was too dirty. It's true, the workers are very dirty; they're covered with gray and their hands are dry and cracked.

I understand that 590,000 tons of debris has been removed from the site and there are 1.2 million tons left to remove. Those are masses I cannot even comprehend. Sometimes when I am sitting with the workers they pull out their tiny tubes of cream, which we pass out at the supply table. As we talk they rub the cream on their hands. Almost automatically, they lean over the pew to share, squeezing some onto my hands; I always take it.

The chemicals around the site and the quality of the air are quite drying. Maybe that's why I too have cracked skin on my hands and yet do no physical work. The podiatrist once made a big deal of bandaging my thumb and one of my fingers that were both bleeding slightly. I was very accepting of his Neosporin treatment, wanting neither to get nor pass germs. He joked about how much education it had required to enable him to do such a good job on my hand with a Band-Aid and some extra white surgical tape. All of the volunteers are just great. Later that same day, the same ironworker came in again. When he saw me he said, "Now you can shake my hand. The President of the United States just shook my hand. He shook MY hand, out on the site."

Of course I shook his hand again and acted as though it were a huge deal. The grin on his face went from ear to ear. But then I told him that it had been just as much an honor to shake his hand that morning. He has his job to do, I have my job to do, and the President has his job to do. I told him that we are all just people and, underneath, all exactly the same. I shook his hand again saying, "I am privileged to shake YOUR hand."

While walking through the Red Cross Respite center, I had noticed a big sign in the front: Friends of Bill W. Meeting 24 hours a day in room 221. I was glad to see it.

For those of us in the general public some information came on the news today saying that there will be 34% more incidence of depression than usual, 35% more incidence of Post Traumatic Stress Syndrome and 40% more abuse of alcohol as a coping mechanism as a result of the events of 9/11. It scares me to think about the stress these policemen, firemen, construction workers, steelworkers, ironworkers, and machinery operators are under.

I am thankful that Alcoholics Anonymous is one of the ministries being offered at the site. I remember that it was at St. Paul in Goldsboro where, as staff, I was first put in charge of all of the twelve-step groups. It was really the first time that I had read through the literature and studied all of the twelve steps. It dawned on me at the time that this was Wesley's Ordo Salutus (Order of Salvation). I thought, hey, Bill W. stole John Wesley's Ordo Salutus for his twelve steps! But then as the years went by, I realized there is no other order of salvation (Salvation: wholeness, wellness, completeness, joyfulness, peace in this life and completed in the next.) First we must acknowledge what keeps us from receiving salvation, next we must admit we are not able to take care of it by ourselves, then allow God to work in us . . . and so on. It's wonderful that, 24 hours a day, workers can go to AA on the inside of the barricade and find others, who have gone before in their exact steps, to lead and walk with them.

At times, I can't help thinking about the plane crash, another 266 people dead and a city already mourning seeks to understand. One of the chaplains, whom I met before when I was here in October, is retired clergy, a licensed family therapist, and a corporate coach. He is a great guy and we bonded with shared tears from the last time. He agreed to serve as chaplain for the plane crash morgue. There is no one more qualified to be there. However, at our first nightly debriefing session he was obviously shaken when he told of his experiences with the upset morgue workers.

My chaplain friend shared that the hardest thing for him that day had been dealing with the workers who had opened one body bag and found a young woman, still strapped into her plane seat, clutching her infant child tightly against her body. He cried, I cried, we all cried.

Can there be a more powerful symbol? In the worst of times, war, biochemical attack, terrorists, valleys of pain, loneliness, and a wilderness of emptiness, nothing can separate us from the arms of LOVE . . . nothing . . . especially not death.

A Pastor's Journal
Entry Twenty-Five - NYC - Ground Zero
November 19, 2001

Two of my "regulars" came in, about seven p.m., looking exhausted. (They call me Miss North Carolina . . . it's a joke we all smile about.)

They said, "Haven't you missed us today?"

I grinned and said, "Of course, I've been standing at the door all day, just waiting for you!"

They got their food sat down in the back pew, where they always sit. I sat in the pew in front and turned to face them. "You guys look pooped."

"Yep, this is our first break today."

"Oh my gosh, no morning break, no lunch break, no afternoon break."

"No."

They had been working all day, trying to make a totally unsafe building safe to work in. They climbed up fifty-five floors carrying all of the gear and tools the cranes couldn't get up there. After the harrowing climb, they had to do the work. They rested as I waited on them hand-and-foot and teased them about having to wash their dishes (everything is paper and plastic). One of them told me of the construction of the WTC building. He told me we should have seen this terrorist attack coming after suffering the attack several years before. "But, we fooled them with our construction," he added. "They thought that they could knock over the towers by flying the planes into them. The effect would have been that the entire lower part of Manhattan would have been destroyed. The whole Financial District would have been lost, if those two towers had toppled over. Instead they were built to implode. One floor just collapsed on the other compacting them perfectly all the way down. That's why the guys digging are now working in sub-basement three (three floors of seven below ground level) but they are removing debris from the fiftieth floor."

"WOW!" was my only reaction.

The conversation covered many subjects related to their work. I asked about their present level of exhaustion; the first worker said that they would get used to it. The other worker said that here working twelve hours on and having twelve off wasn't bad. He told me about his working on the steel on the Disney World Project, where, nearby they had beds, showers, and fresh uniforms to put on. So there they would work twelve, sleep four, shower, and then do another twelve, around the clock. I already suspected the answer to the question of why they would do such a crazy thing. It's the money, of course.

Money is the root of many of problems. The majority of times, when couples come for counseling the issues are of sexual intimacy, children, or MONEY. It seems that people view the world from two opposing perspectives: abundance or scarcity. Often I ask couples or individuals how much will be enough. They can come up with a figure but when they reach it, it's still not enough. From my perspective, whatever one has at the moment is a gracious abundance.

I've been wealthy and I've been poor (now neither . . . thank goodness) and my happiness was never dependent upon my net worth. It may only be coincidence but I was much happier and more peaceful while poor. One of my greatest memories is working in tobacco in May of '75 (I thought I would die after the first fifteen minutes, bent over in the field, pulling plants from the bedding fields! But I didn't). It was get just enough extra money to send both children to camp for a week. I learned a great lesson that May, when I asked my boss, "Mr. Poole, exactly what percentage of these tobacco plants do you expect to live?"

He said, "One hundred percent of them, Camille, one hundred percent."

That's the way I see it with people. Who on this earth is to be loved into wholeness, completeness, joyfulness, health, etc ? ONE HUNDRED PERCENT, EVERY SINGLE ONE.

Back to the two ironworkers; on top of everything else, the day before, the police had towed one's car for being in the path of President Bush. After a long exhausting day, it took him an hour and a half extra to find his car and start back to his hotel in New Jersey. These two really needed to be heard. The thanks the workers give me is unreal. I listen as they tell about their families; the young ones show me pictures of their children, which they have taped on the inside tops of their hats. It's so obvious they have less time for life than I have. Listening to the workers is important to me. I hope I'm doing it for them, not for me.

There is a huge theological difference in how the Episcopalians interact with the workers and how I do. The first morning I walked in, the Father told me that this was a ministry of presence and we were not here to proselytize or preach. I concurred and assured him that I understood; he wouldn't have to worry about me proselytizing. All of the sisters (no they don't live in a nunnery, Camille, it's called a convent) and the priests are very recognizable in their full clerics. I expect that everyone is NEEDY. I have never met anyone in my life who doesn't have skeletons in their closet, sadness in their family, and some pain in their hearts. I hope that my engaging everyone in conversation doesn't make priest think I am too pushy. They all seem very responsive to conversation.

There were four police officers from California who had come here for the purpose of saving souls. They presented a problem because although their ministry was not one merely of presence, police are allowed in here and they had come from California. Their style turned my stomach but, hey, in God's world there is room for all. They have gone home now. Their hearts are in the right place; they're really nice guys.

The first person I spoke with on my first trip was also one of the last I spoke with. I remember his name because someone who is no longer in our family has the same name. Hmmm, people do move in and out of families these days. He has a very round, smiley face, very short light brown hair, and a burly physique.

This last time, he came with someone who is six inches taller and really bulky, with a light beard. They sat together and began eating.

I approached, called his name and said, "Hey, who's your friend?" The friend introduced himself and I introduced myself.

My smiley-faced worker punched him in the ribs with his elbow and grinned, saying, "I told you this was the best place to come. Not only do they have the best food, they have the friendliest volunteers." He winked.

His friend began telling about his job driving the largest crane on the pit.

"Yes," I said, "I have seen the three yellow cranes on TV."

"I'm the one flying the flags." He looked me in the eye and said, "I don't have one from North Carolina. I'll bet you could get me one. I fly them on the tall arm that holds the basket that he (he tilted his head toward his friend) rides in up to the top of those buildings."

Instantly I got huge tears in my eyes and I looked at my smiley-faced friend and said, "You never told me you are the one at the top of that huge crane."

Very childlike, he said, "I didn't want you to worry. I don't want you to cry either, here." He handed me his napkin. "I'll be fine," he continued. "I know what I'm doing."

His comments only reinforced my knowledge of how dangerous his job really is. Most of the officers and construction workers tell me that they don't tell their wives about what really goes on in their jobs because it would be too difficult for them to handle. In fact, one of the young Army men that was on his way to Afghanistan told me he hadn't even told his parents that the six-month deployment had been pushed to one month earlier. He said, "They worry enough. I just want to give them as much worry-free time as possible. I'll call them the day before we ship out."

There were a couple of reasons for tears in my eyes (I didn't need his napkin . . . they didn't roll out of my eyes.) One reason is that these people are doing highly dangerous jobs out there. The whole site is dangerous; glass dangles from partially shattered windows sixty stories up, massive steel girders hang by steel shards. The ground gave way and one of the smaller grapplers fell three stories into the hole. All the guys were talking about it when they came in. The site is unstable and highly dangerous; it's as simple as that.

Following the collapse, several of the workers were taken to the hospital but miraculously no one was critically hurt. I heard that all but one was back on the site in a couple of hours. Another reason for the tears was that I knew I would be leaving and perhaps not seeing these people again. They nearly always ask when they leave, "See you tomorrow?" Bonding takes place pretty fast here. It's as in a hospital or at a wedding or family funeral. I may spend only a few hours with them but one of the special parts of being a pastor is that I spend time with people at crucial and transitional times in their lives. Under such circumstances, bonding is pretty quick and usually lasts forever.

Leaving these workers will be bittersweet. It will be good to get home but difficult to leave these people who are each now a part of my life.

I am concerned about the crane operator. He has worked twelve hours on, seven days a week, every single day but Veterans Day. He told me he would also work Thanksgiving. It seems as though they will all be working Thanksgiving. I really should try to get him a flag from North Carolina. Dan Gearino of the Raleigh News and Observer will be doing a story on my ministry up here in NYC the first week in December. They even sent a photographer with me from the New York Times. Even with many phone calls, he could not get into St. Paul's to take pictures. Maybe Dan can get me a flag. It would be nice to have NC flying over the pit. It would be one more of many symbols that we are all in this together.

A Pastor's Journal
Entry Twenty-Six - Raleigh
Thanksgiving, 2001

I'm thankful to be spending Thanksgiving at home with Mother, my four children, three grandchildren (okay, they are step, in fact, they're ex-step but who's into details?), and a couple extras; always we have extras. The young army guys I invited, in case they were in Fayetteville before being deployed, did not come or call. Maybe they have already gone to Afghanistan, perhaps they couldn't leave, or maybe they couldn't even make a phone call.

Everyone brought a dish but, as usual, we spent most of the day in the kitchen anyway. Since 1985, I have had my thanksgiving dinner at the noon meal so that Julie and Cris could go on to their mother's house for her family meal. It works out fine, especially today because I'm pooped and now everyone is gone.

We didn't decorate the cake until two a.m. this morning, amid much laughter. We made half with coconut and half without since the kids don't like coconut. Tyson even made a smiley face with Oreo cookies on the WITHOUT half. I'm afraid we're not terribly reverent on what are supposed to be formal dinner occasions. At the bottom of the cake-making directions, Cris read, "Keep iced four-layer cake (Julie got a large charge out of slicing the two layers in half using a thread and did a great job) in the refrigerator for three days before serving." All of the kids roared with laughter at that advice, since it was two .a.m. on Thanksgiving morning.

Cris said loudly, "Camille, what were you doing three days ago when you were supposed to be making our Thanksgiving Cake?"

Gee, I must be falling down on my motherly duties. I laughed as loudly as I ever have at the thought of having to plan a cake three days in advance. No one on a deathbed ever says, "I wish my cake had been perfect for Thanksgiving," but they may say, "I wish I had laughed more with my children." This Thanksgiving, I'm thankful for a cake made at two a.m. by a loving family. I'm thankful for that cake eaten three days too soon, or made three days too late, but made with love, laughter, and a lot of imperfections! I'm pooped but it is a good pooped.

It's now several days after Thanksgiving and I find that it's much harder to be focused enough to write here at home in Raleigh. It isn't that I don't have just as many thoughts, it's just that I'm so easily distracted. Rachel and Uk helped me move my office yesterday, out of my bedroom and up into the library. The library is where my office is supposed to be but when I got sick, last year, I wanted my computer by my bed. Now my bedroom is free from office stuff and clutter and I know uncluttered sleep is precious. Clutter anywhere in the house upsets me and keeps me from focusing and from being my best self. Feng Shui principles say unless you love it, or use it, toss it.

My bedroom may be uncluttered but that's not enough. On my way to the library, towels from Thanksgiving needing to be moved from washer to dryer and sheets needing to be folded out of the dryer waylaid me. I got hot and decided to put on sandals, only to realize that, in order to wear sandals, I needed to take off my cracked and pealed toenail polish. Since I have a meeting at two p.m. today concerning the new faith community, Hope in the Wilderness, I decide I had better do my hair and put on some make up. Oh, the cat needs a pill for that abscess.

The phone rings. It's Webmaster Jack asking why I haven't finished writing the last two articles that I told him days ago were almost finished (don't even think about the 250 e-mails that I'd like to answer). The dog's scratching; I should put something in her ear again. I need to unload the dishwasher. If I'm going to be in the library, I need a cord for the phone to plug in up there. I need to put a little WD-40 on the rollers for the keyboard drawer. I need to clean up those two spots on the stairs; the grandchildren must have spilled a little over Thanksgiving. Did I get yesterday's mail? No, Camille, go get the mail.

On the way to the mailbox I notice that I need to cut back the Impatiens that froze on Thanksgiving morning. It's interesting they all didn't freeze. It was only the tall beautiful ones. The shorter ones closer to the ground are still blooming at the end of November. Hmmm, I wish there really were consequences like that for being tall and beautiful . . . tacky, Camille, tacky. They do always seem so perfect.

I remember one shopping trip to Atlanta with one of my good friends. We were getting dressed to see (again) Phantom of the Opera. We were standing in front of the bathroom mirror putting on make up, when I said, "It's totally intimidating to stand beside you and put on make up. Look at you. You're so gorgeous (I might add, she had also been a model). Her response was so profound, I have always remembered it, "Camille, I had nothing to do with how I look. I was born this way. It's what we make of ourselves that's important not how we look."

Of course, I knew that, she was right. However, I'm still not sad to see that the tall and beautiful flowers were frozen and the short, squatty ones will still be here and blooming well into December.

As I cut away all of the frozen Impatiens I couldn't help thinking all the while about the funeral I preached for my mother-in-law, ex-mother-in-law that is, who died on September 13. I saw her death as similar to the cycle of the flower bloom. In the cycle, the flower dies and falls to the ground in order that life may rise again in the spring, a new plant, blooming again, often more beautiful and complete than that of the previous year. I spoke of the different ways she had bloomed throughout her life. We definitely celebrated death and resurrection. Anyway, into the compost went the TALL BEAUTIFUL (but frozen and dead) flowers.

There are always distractions but they seem to be more abundant or stronger when I first return from New York; it's that way too when I first get there.   There, after a brief period of adjustment, I have not much more to do than to work and write. Here there is a whole busy life.

I think about the woman who was always sitting at the top of the stairs when I got off the train at 59th and Lexington and came up the steps out of the subway station by Bloomingdale's. She has one of those tall shopping carts (two story). It's loaded down with messy, black plastic garbage bags stuffed and overflowing. Probably all she has in the whole world. She always has on her coat, even when it is hot. She does not beg, nor does she have a can or a box for donations. She always seems busy doing something but I have no idea what. It is definitely her spot. She is always there. The first few times I walked past, I tried not to look at her. To be honest, I have to say that I ignored her completely. Some time later she had become a familiar fixture and I would look, then nod. The last few times, I'd smile a greeting and she would nod but she did not smile.   I guess those who regularly come up her stairs become her community. She has no distractions. Her world is very simple. I wonder where she goes to the bathroom?

A dear old friend of mine called the other day to say he liked reading my journal. He was quite complementary, but he added, "Your picture is terrible. You don't look like I remember you. You look old. I like the picture I have of you in high school (duh . . . that was forty years ago!)" Anyway, I still feel the same age on the inside. His attitude is fairly typical for a lot of people who choose to live in the past. He is my age and thinks the title of that book by Tom Brockaw, *The*

World's Greatest Generation, about the WWII generation, is right on. He knows nothing of the TV programs *Sex in the City* or *Alley McBeal*. I guess it's fine for some to live in the past, liking old music, (listens to Lawrence Welk???)   But when Moses was talking to God at the burning bush and asked God to give a name so that Moses could tell the people what to call God, God said, "Tell them I AM; my name is I AM." God did not tell Moses to tell the people, "I WAS." That is the present tense of the verb "to be," NOT past tense, not future tense either. God did not tell Moses my name is, "I SHALL BE"

It is so hard for some people to live in the present moment. Some dream about future castles and then try to live there. Others forever want things to be the way they were. I've had parishioners who described what their houses were like before they retired (over and over) or what their family used to do (over and over again). Some people are addicted to telling how wonderful times were in the olden days, when values were this way, morals were that way, and families were this way and so forth, but it is now not then! God is the God of the present, however it looks and however it is!!! Our God whose name is I AM. The present is perfect just as it is.

It is very difficult for some people to change or accept change. I understand that mother birds often begin making their nests quite uncomfortable with briars and sticky things so that the little birds are forced to fly out of the nest to get away from the discomfort. No one makes a change until the pain of changing becomes less than the pain of staying in the same place.   Some people must become too numb or too accustomed to the sticky, poky nests of the past, otherwise they would fly out. I'm willing to go with the flow of the times. Personally, I believe my children are the perfect generation. Why? Because it is the one they have. Mine is the perfect generation as well, if I choose to live in this world with them. No matter what I am going through, no matter what my distractions, this moment is perfect for me. It is perfect for the bag lady as well, sitting at the top of the stairs. Why? Because this is the moment we have . . . personally, I believe it perfect that only the tall beautiful flowers were frozen!!!

I'll be going back to New York about the second week in December, I think. I must check the schedule with St. Paul's, the Red Cross, and the New York Conference. I miss the people I met there. For me, they became community. It makes me sad to think that I may never see some of them again. For the time being, I'm grateful for the story that I am living now, each day. I'm trying to really savor every moment. I am thankful in this week of Thanksgiving for my ordinary life. I am thankful for ministry in NYC, and the lives that have touched mine. I am thankful for my ordinary family, my cat who purrs right beside my ear each night, friends who offer support and prayers, wonderful red and yellow leaves of fall covering the yard, my dog who won't let me out of her sight, and for the privilege of being able to turn on the heat and run the air conditioner on the same day, if I want to. I am thankful that I am able to recognize what a blessed life I live.

A Pastor's Journal
Entry Twenty-Seven - NYC - Ground Zero
December 12, 2001

There is always the hustle and bustle of closing up the house before taking a trip. Thank goodness I took my dog, Airlie (named for Airlie Gardens in Wilmington), to her "grandmother's house" on Monday night! Then it's time to fill the automatic water and feeder machines for the cat, stop the mail, set the thermostat, water the plants, put the lights on timers, wash the final couple of loads of wash, decide what to take (the biggest job of the day!!!) and pack not only clothes but computer stuff, ya da, ya da. As I was painstakingly making my hair look perfect (Bob used to say that if I spent as much time on my body as I did my hair, I'd be a whole lot happier), I realized it would only be a few hours until it was all under a hard hat anyway.

Tonight I will be working all night in what is called T-MORT. It is the temporary morgue used inside the barriers at Ground Zero. When I called the Red Cross, to state my availability, my friend there said, "Go check the color of your Red Cross ID."

Returning to the phone, I told her, "It's green."

"Oh wonderful, you have *full* access!" she said in her slight British accent, "They found fourteen bodies yesterday and we need you to work on site. Can you do that?"

Of course I can and will. I called another chaplain in Florida to ask what I was supposed to do there. He told me that from the moment a body is found, through all of the procedures on site, until the ambulance takes it to D-MORT, the permanent disaster morgue at the hospital, the chaplain is in charge of the body and must be beside it at all times, saying appropriate responses for the Catholic workers and firefighters and prayers for the person's life and the relatives who will perhaps now have some peace.

I said, of course, all of that sounds familiar. However, I did once again feel a huge lump in my throat. What an honor it is to accompany the body of a real person who lived a real life with a real family and died in the worst disaster in American History. I am truly blessed to be able to walk with those who are actually doing the difficult work of recovery. It really doesn't matter what my hair looks like or even my body for that matter.

This intimate opportunity is really human-to-human, soul-to-soul or spirit-to-spirit. What an honor to work all night in such a capacity. A year ago I was too sick to do even this and now . . .

This is my fifth time to fly since September 11, 2001. Yes, it is still strange to see the National Guard in camouflage uniforms with M-16s standing at the end of the security walk-through. It's a pain in the neck to undo computer bags and be at the airport two hours early (Rachel took me and it was nice to spend that thirty-minute ride with her), but the increased security is necessary, especially today. It's the last day of Ramadan, the Muslim holidays, and the United States is expecting more violence. It's a holy time and some misguided Muslims think it a privilege to die on such days as martyrs. President Bush is going to release the tape of Bin Laden bragging that he is the one who planned the attack on the World Trade Center, but I won't see it since I'll be flying. Evidently in the tape, he says he is surprised that the floors below the air attack were destroyed (so much for the theory that he was trying to knock them down).

My plane is a tiny jet. I love tiny jets—firstly because they aren't very crowded because people are afraid to fly on them (today only eleven people) and, secondly, I can pretend that it's a private jet, a flying limo just for me. Since they don't carry much fuel, it isn't likely they would be used as crash bombers.

The flight was uneventful, but one gets much more motion in the small planes. I've ridden in several planes smaller than this. One of my members at St. Paul UMC in Goldsboro flew my library and me to my next church. Also, I would fly with Herb Stout to finance meetings from Ocean Isle (we took off from a field, literally). Once, after church, from that same grass field airport, I was flown to Raleigh to perform a wedding for a good friend. I really didn't think we were going to make it that time—the turbulence was terrible. I used to fly with another friend on his personal plane out of the Durham airport for fun rides to Goldsboro. On one fun ride, the Seymour Johnson air traffic controller told us to get out of military airspace immediately. We did. I've taken the controls a little, making the plane go up and down, but not much. It was truly a shock when I learned that Herb Stout was killed in his own plane.

Arriving in La Guardia was wonderful. It felt like coming home. Seeing and hearing all the familiar sites and sounds was comforting. I felt like a true New Yorker when, after I got my bags, a man in a dark suit stopped and asked me if I wanted a cab. I answered in the affirmative, but quickly asked if it was a yellow cab.

He said, "No, a Lincoln."

I said, "No thank you."

He said, "Yes, everything same as yellow cab."

"What's the fare?"

"Forty dollars plus bags."

"Hell no! A legal yellow cab is twenty dollars plus bags." I stomped off to get a real cab.

It made me angry because such drivers aren't registered, have no insurance, rip off the unsuspecting and don't play fair. They come inside the airport and take fares away from the legitimate drivers who wait patiently (okay, not so patiently) outside for fares. The cabby today told me he waited in line last night for three hours and had not one fare, so he gave up and went home. I felt sorry for him.

The economy up here is hurting so badly. On the plane, I read in the newspaper that the businesses are hurting so badly in the financial district that there is a sign outside of a barbershop with a picture of a bald man sitting in the chair getting a hair cut, the print says, "He doesn't need it, but we do."

Driving into town, we saw a huge banner hanging from a thirty-story penthouse balcony that proclaimed "God Bless America" and a building whose whole side was painted as an American flag. The glorious holiday lights are everywhere. The people here in NYC are really trying to put on a happy face and recover in the aftermath of the terrorist attack.

Yesterday as I was dreading coming back to my dingy little hotel room. I called the manager of the hotel.

"Hi, this is Camille Yorkey and I'm coming up to work with UMCOR."

"Hi Camille, I remember you. I cashed a check for you in my office the first time you came. You only had two dollars in your pocket and said, 'Don't tell my mother.'" He laughed.

"Yes, well, I'm coming up tomorrow for my third trip with UMCOR. I want to know exactly how much extra the few friends and churches, who are paying my expenses to volunteer, will have to pay for me to have a bathroom."

"Don't worry. I'll take care of it. Just don't tell any of the other volunteers about it."

I'm so glad I asked about a change. Maybe I did it because the subject at my CIC women's spiritual growth group this week was Believing you Deserve the Best . . . WOW and was I ever thankful we had that chapter this week.

When I walked in today, the manager said, "HI, it's Yorkey, right?"

"Yes." Well, I feel as if I have died and gone to heaven—wish I were staying a month. However, that's just because everything is relative.

This room has two light bulbs and one is over the unbroken mirror. There is a stopper in the sink, which makes washing underwear much easier. I have two windows; one looks straight up Lexington Avenue, and I can see the Christmas trees on top of Bloomingdales!!! I have a queen size bed. Even though I share the bath, it's only with the room next door and we each have a door so I don't have to go into the hall to get there. I have a TV with a channel flipper AND a CLOCK. It feels like the Ritz! That's good because, this time, my schedule is grueling—three twelve-hour shifts at St. Paul's, three nights at T-MORT, plus the time I must devote to writing.

I must run. I have to get a pass for the subway trains and get down to ground zero with my hard hat, Red Cross vest, coat, gloves and scarf. It's cold and the wind is blowing. Down on the street a man is standing with his saxophone and coming through my OPEN window is the sweet sounds of Hark the Herald Angels Sing. We each do what we can. I know I'm here to do what I can do, where God has called me to be. Still, I'm a bit nervous.

A Pastor's Journal
Entry Twenty-Eight - NYC - Ground Zero
December 13, 2001

The difficulties in having to spend the entire night in T-MORT inside the barricade at Ground Zero for the first time come from having to face the unknown. The first difficult thing was thinking about it, the second was forcing myself to walk through the site alone to get there, and the third difficult thing was stepping into the morgue. As my friend Nancy always says, "Do it afraid." Once inside, I knew exactly why I was there and what I was supposed to do.

More bodies were recovered yesterday than any other day so far. Basically I preached ten to fifteen mini-funerals. Because it's a crime scene, the T-MORT supervisor is a NYPD forensic detective and I'm not permitted to talk to anyone about the details. Nor will anyone working in the morgue be permitted to work with any families of those killed. That was new information for me but it's understandable.

It was my first trip into the site alone after dark. It's amazing how the bright lights make the whole scene an eerie shade of gray . . . almost silver. As I walk under the lights I remember chatting with the workers who keep this site lighted. They are so proud of their 24-7 difficult job of keeping the lights running. Up close, one can see the brown color of the dirt, mud, debris and crumpled steel; however, from the barricades it looks as though cinematographers have put gossamer over a lens to make everything appear as a gray winter scene from *Dr. Zhivago*.

The pungent smell is always the same. People can often recognize their surroundings or environment by distinctive odors, and I will always recognize Ground Zero. It has a unique odor all its own, and the air seems thick somehow. In the brilliant lights, small particles are always visible floating around, suspended in and moving with the air. Tonight, one firefighter told me that the center of the rubble mass is still 1200-1300 degrees. Fires break out often. Everything stays wet from the fire hoses and looks heavy. Tonight it is raining a slight drizzle; the hard hat is good for that.

I have mixed feelings here at the site. I feel it is all so horrible, terrible, morbid, cruel, sad, and every other negative sentiment. Yet I know that out of the rubble new life comes. People across the world are reaching out to hug the ones they love; more people are no longer finding reasons to delay their getting married; people are seeking the true meaning of their lives; there is more solidarity among the people in the country; and perhaps the most powerful change of all is the people's hunger for God which has grown from this terrorist attack.

God's presence is very evident and can be felt everywhere around and at Ground Zero. The area is a temporary burial ground, and it is being treated as holy by all those privileged to work here.   The people working here are exceptional, all doing their part well, unbelievably well—their hands are God's hands. Everyone here seems to know instinctively what to do.

They are exhausted and yet continue to work under unbelievable difficult conditions. They are about to reach total mental and physical exhaustion. Here, everyone is what he or she needs to be, doing their own small part of this monumental task. This is truly holy ground.

People still stand at the barricades and weep; perhaps they are seeing it for the first time. When I took a break at midnight, there was a group of six in formal attire—tuxes and cocktail dresses (the men had scarves around their necks . . . I love that look!). It was obvious they were either coming from or going to a Christmas party nearby. However, they had no champagne. They were somber as they read the many posters, letters, and signs in front of St. Paul's.

It is remarkable that tonight I became one of the volunteers to whom those at St. Paul were ministering. It's fascinating how things come full circle. I ate dinner at St. Paul's and listened to several oboe and piano Christmas duets before going back on duty.

T-MORT is divided into two rooms and we wait in the front room until the dead are brought in. Tonight there were always two teams of EMT-Certified Firefighters working under one leader. A police officer was on duty at the front door and another at the back.

When the bodies are brought into T-MORT there are as many as fifteen individuals present in the back room for the service, or mini-funeral; I think I'll just call it a blessing with prayer.

At the first blessing, it became immediately obvious to the others that I was different from those they were accustomed to.

The EMT leader came up to me and said, "Wow, that was great, you sounded like you really knew the person. Do you always 'wing it' like that?"

"Uh oh, what did I do wrong?" I asked her.

"Well, most of the priests just read stuff."

I asked her if I should read the same stuff. She said no.

I remember going to an Episcopal funeral in Goldsboro for a high school girl who had been killed on New Year's Eve. She was a friend of all four of my children. It was terrible loss. It shocked me that nothing was ever said about her in the funeral service. There is merit in the theology that we all are equal, that it doesn't matter who we are or what we did or didn't do, but I feel that we are all different and God's unique creations. At the WTC temporary morgue I tried to do each blessing a little differently, but always with the assurance of God's love for the individual and with the assurance each spirit has been with God since the terrible day of September 11.

Over the course of the night, I had a chance to speak of the lives of those who died with the gifts they had been given by God, about their families and friends who love them, the joys and sorrows they experienced in their lifetimes, the closure, and the peace that finding these bodies will hopefully bring to the families. I had a chance to say that although we don't understand why this terrible thing happened or how this work we are now doing will help, we do understand that God's love is NEVER failing, no matter what. I spoke of our assurance of life after death and how we must celebrate the life they have lived and shared. I spoke of the diligent work of the on-site workers and their meticulous recovery efforts.

As I gave the blessings, I felt it very important to remember and use my traditional Trinitarian language, but I had no idea what theological discussions might arise from my brief "eulogies and prayers."

One chaplain, who had a very abbreviated duty at T-MORT, had prayed that we have no assurance the victim was "saved," and no one knows what fate waited. His words upset those present so greatly that he was immediately removed from Ground Zero.

I've thought about such theology a great deal. We all know people who may believe that we can't know a particular person's fate but how exactly does that theology help the living? I believe it's a cruel theology. What kind of a minuscule God would be so petty? My God is a God of grace, love, forgiveness, life, and abundance, and on, and on . . .

The most bizarre thought to come to me all night was that I might very well be praying for one of the hijackers. Even so, it is not for me to judge these individuals but for God.

Everything I said I believe to be true, regardless of for whom I was praying. We cannot judge one another by some arbitrary scale—it's bad to lie, but worse to steel, worse to commit adultery, worse to be bigoted, worse to hate, worse to hit, worse to kill, worse to believe in a cause enough to go to war . . . and so on. Those who witnessed the prayers and words for the dead had their own varying thoughts and beliefs. They are so young, and inquisitive.

One young firefighter said, "If you had a church here, I'd come and I don't go anywhere now."

Those words were precious to my ears but made me sad. We must meet the needs of these young people. They are all in their twenties and thirties. The youngest woman in T-MORT tonight is 22, with a three-year-old and four-month-old at home. She has two little ones at home and yet she is working through the night with me in T-MORT. Bless her heart.

The shift changed while I was there and I had the opportunity to work with different teams of firefighters, police, and EMTs. It was the first time I had ever worked beside a medical examiner (M.E.), and it might have been terrifying if I had not read all of Patricia Cornwell's books. Even so, I did not know exactly what to expect.

At one point I said, "The only assurance we have after we are born is of dying but we just never know when or how that will occur." We really should talk more about death in our society because it is such a natural part of life. Some widows I know wear that title as a distinction, like a badge. I just tell them that everyone in the world who is married will become widowed at some point. (Unless they die first—smile)

As I was speaking of birth, I remembered that as I rode from the airport today the taxicab passed the Manhattan School of Science and Math. In Durham, the old Watts Hospital has become the North Carolina School of Science and Math. Both Rachel and Tyson were born in that building. I was such a hippy back then. They were both delivered by natural childbirth or what then was called hypnosis.

Randy was with me when both Rachel and Tyson were born, which was quite rare in late sixties and early seventies. We carried Rachel out of the delivery room to the nursery. When Tyson was born we had the same room, number 301, a corner room on the third floor of Old Watts Hospital—now the School of Science and Math. I may be one of the few who loved being pregnant, loved delivering my two babies, loved nursing them—absolutely adore them now. However, there were a few times in between that I could have killed all four of them. At one point I even told Tyson, "Hey, its you or me. One of us has to go." I'm glad those days are long gone.

My precious Tyson is spending the night on the floor of his new store in Wilmington tonight. He's the manager and the store is not quite finished. His product came but the alarm system is not yet installed, so he's there protecting everything. Boy is his company fortunate to have such a loyal, dependable, and responsible manager.

Sometimes it seems only yesterday that my children were born, other times so far away as to be in another lifetime. Birth and death, both so sacred, so precious, both a transition from what has been to what will be. I hope the families will somehow feel or come to know that their loved ones, who were lost so tragically, are still loved. I pray that someday their tears will turn to new life just as each of these who pass through this holy ground.

A Pastor's Journal
Entry Twenty-Nine - NYC - Ground Zero
December 14, 2001

It is cool to be back on the eleventh floor, the same floor where my room was on the first trip in October. I have the same maid, Maria. When we saw each other today we hugged. Even though she speaks only Spanish, I somehow understood that she was glad that I am back and now have a room that is "bonito," much more bonito than the other one. I told her how happy I am to be here and to have her here too.

I had to Feng Shui my room; the layout would never do. I asked Maria to please help me turn the pillows to the foot of the bed and to put the bed on a different wall. She said she remembered my rearranging the other room also. I gave her two dollars. She really didn't want to take it but I forced her, saying that it was a Christmas present. It made her very happy—such a small thing—not much of a present. Last time, I needed a chair and the guy downstairs was more than happy to take $10 for just getting me a chair. I'll give Maria $10 also to find me a chair; I'm sure she needs it. It kills my back to type from my bed as I did on the first trip. After she left, I moved all three pieces of furniture.

The reason I had to turn the bed was for the feeling of safety—you should always be able to see the door (you know, so the "terrors" can't get in). Also, for protection a turtle's shell, e.g. a wall, should be behind the bed. A bed should never be in the middle of a room. Such an arrangement really works;

children and adults sleep better with the protection of a
"turtle shell" at their backs. Just moving the beds around
makes everyone feel safer.

More good news—I don't share my bathroom. There is a door
to the other room, but it's locked with a key and the couple on
the other side of the door goes down the hall to a bath, I
guess. I hugged the manager today. I told him I was so very
happy with my room and that it was beautiful—thank you,
thank you, thank you. He is a large man and has a thick accent,
dark hair, and mustache, and his is an old country last
name—De "something."

He returned my hug, smiled, and said, "You are welcome, Miss
Yorkey."

Imagine being called "Miss" at my age. It felt nice.

Coming home in the middle of the night wasn't so bad last
night. The subways are brightly lighted and many people were
riding them. I was glad that I know my way around on them
much better now. I fell asleep on the train and woke up with
a start. I asked the lovely woman next to me, "Where are we?
What stop is this?"

She said, "Where are you going?"

I told her 59th. She smiled. "Go back to sleep, I'll wake you
when we get there."

I did and she did.

At the top of the stairs at the Bloomingdale's stop, I discovered that the woman wasn't there for the very first time. Where was she? Had something happened to her? But then, I thought that maybe she sleeps somewhere else when it is cold. After all, it was the first time I had come up the steps so late.

Bloomingdale's on Lexington Avenue is just a couple of blocks from my hotel. The decorated display windows are beautiful. As I walked along the sidewalk I marveled at all the moving parts of the displays, and in front of me was a gorgeous view with the magnificent Chrysler Building at the end of Lexington. I am a blessed human indeed.

Although impressive, the windows didn't seem quite as exciting as I remember those at Woodies in Washington DC when I was a child. Every year, Mother and Daddy used to take my brother and me into the city to see the windows late at night, when most traffic had gone and we could drive by very slowly. It was one of the highlights of the Christmas season. We couldn't believe that they could make such complex figurines, in full holiday garb, move around in the store windows as they did.

Things change. When we grow up things come into perspective. With the whole world now being motorized, computerized, and animated, the holiday windows don't hold the same fascination they once did. In addition, for me now, it's not quite the same—not a family outing—I'm alone. However, they are colorful and festive, and I do get to gaze at them as long as I wish. There are no crowds vying for position at the windows at this time of night, to better see the displays.

I've discovered that I cannot take the restrooms for granted while working in the morgue at Ground Zero. Last night, after drinking two bottles of water I was in need of a restroom. St. Paul's was five blocks away. When I asked someone where I could find one, he pointed toward a porta-potty. It seems that all the people inside the barricades use them. It was ten or eleven p.m. and had been dark since 4:30. There are no lights in those big blue boxes—oh well. Just as I put my hand on the door handle, I heard, "Camille, is that you?"

I turned and in the dark could just make out the shape of a police officer coming toward me.

He said, "It's Mike. I just was talking to you in the morgue. I came in to warm up by the heater; remember?"

"Oh yes."

"Don't go in there. That is NO place for a lady. Come with me; we'll find you a clean place to go to the bathroom."

He walked me to a street I recognized as the one on the south side, where I had first seen the trucks haul out loads of steel after being hosed off. We entered one of the big buildings just on the inside of the barricades, one that had been spared.

He said, "There's a night watchman around here somewhere." He called out and the watchman quickly came. The watchman wouldn't let me in before he examined my chaplain ID even though I had a police escort.

They both waited outside the door—RIGHT outside the ladies room door—oh well. When the watchman first saw that I was a chaplain he asked if I would pray for him. With a quick smile, I said, "Sure," as I hurried to the bathroom. When I came out, he asked me again. Many people ask but I assume they don't mean right at that minute. I finally realized he meant right then. "Sure I will," I answered. Right there, outside the bathroom, the three of us stood holding hands, made a small circle, and I prayed. I don't remember exactly what I prayed, but it was for all they had been through, for the whole financial district, still terribly crippled from the disaster, for each of us, for the world to be more peaceful this holiday season, for us to be the best that we can be, ya da ya da. I do remember clearly that I ended it with thanks for the bathroom. We all squeezed hands, as if we shared a neat secret. With big smiles we went our separate ways. Mike escorted me back to T-MORT. I am more blessed than anyone can ever understand.

Why on earth did I not think to ask the night watchman exactly what he wished me to pray for? I'm sure he had something in mind or he would not have asked twice. Sometimes I'm just not a very good pastor or counselor or even listener. Every morning I pray to be an instrument of light and grace, then during the busy day my stuff gets in the way and I forget. Why didn't I ask him? Oh, well. He really knows what he needs and so does God. Maybe I'll see him another night.

Last night inside the barricade of Ground Zero ended with hugs to the fire department EMTs and several positive comments from them about the blessings of the bodies and my prayers. I appreciated the comments because I never feel as though I pray very well spontaneously, in public. When someone invites me to pray, I usually decline if anyone else is willing to offer a prayer. I usually say that prayer is for everyone, not just the "professionals." At such times I think, "It's your family, you should pray for them," or "It's your church, you pray for your own church," or "I'm just a guest here, what were you doing for prayer before I came?" It's not at all how preachers are supposed to feel. The motto is "Always be ready to preach, pray or die." Of the three, I'm only ready to DIE spontaneously. I'm definitely ready for that.

I was surprised tonight to find that some working in the temporary morgue, where I was offering blessings for the dead, weren't religious. It must be harder for them to deal with the magnitude of death here than it is for me, because I know in my heart that death is only a graduation into a greater relationship with God.

These folks working in T-MORT weren't chosen because they have an ability to face and deal with death better than their coworkers; they were just called from their other duty in other parts of the city. Though most are from Catholic backgrounds, it seemed that most are not actively practicing; two seemed to have no faith whatsoever.

At first, they were quite leery of me and acted as though they didn't think it necessary to have a chaplain there at all. I could tell by their reluctance to interact with me and to make eye contact. It was somewhat as though I wasn't there to them. . . as if they felt that they were doing all that was really necessary and that I was providing some unneeded garnish.

As the night wore on that attitude changed. We interacted quite a bit and laughed together (yes, even in the morgue, life goes on and laughter is still healing). They asked many questions. One of the two women was very rough and tough acting and seemed a bit older than the rest, maybe in her late thirties, but looked to be older. At first, her brusque manner had intimidated me. As I walked out, saying my goodbyes, she offered no hug and remained seated (she was near the door). She did, however, offer her hand and I shook it.

She lowered her head and said quietly, "Thank you. I liked your stuff tonight, especially your prayers."

I held her hand an extra second. "You are welcome."

Her eyes met mine. It was only for an instant; I could see hers were wet with tears. As I stepped out of T-MORT into the darkness of ground zero, to start my walk back to the train, mine were also.

A Pastor's Journal
Entry Thirty - NYC - Ground Zero
December 15, 2001

Yesterday the Bin Laden tape was released; actually it might have been the day before and I just didn't hear about. It is, I guess, the final straw, knowing for sure that he is the terrorist behind the attacks on the World Trade Center on September 11.

His frivolous demeanor was disgusting. His jovial attitude about how much destruction had been caused and how many innocent lives lost was inhumane and repulsive. However, for me the very worst part of it all was that over fifty times he repeated the phrase "Allah be praised. God be praised." Throughout history too many horrible things have taken place in the name of God. The United States is not exempt from this comment.

Bin Laden is such a perfect example of fundamentalism gone awry. It is one more perfect, sick example of any person or group of people thinking that they are RIGHT which makes everyone else wrong. A pastor of mine from 20 years ago, a dear friend and now the Vice Chair of the Hope in the Wilderness Board of Directors, sent me this quote yesterday.

This says it all:

> "The idea that there is one people in possession
> of the truth, one answer to the world's ills or one

solution to humanity's needs has done untold harm
throughout history." Kofi Annan, UN Sec. Gen, in
a speech on receiving the 2001 Nobel Peace Prize
as quoted in Newsweek Dec. 17, 2001, p. 19.

When, when, oh God, will we begin to realize there is room for
all of us? When will we be able to celebrate our uniqueness
and our differences? We in the Western World are just as
guilty . . . more guilty because we should know better and care
more.

President Bush also pulled the United States out of the
Nuclear Arms Treaty that has been in effect since 1972,
thirty years. How is today different? Every moment we
breathe we are making history. I only pray that we are making
a positive difference in this world's history for our
grandchildren and great- and great-great-grandchildren.

I'm off to St. Paul's for the day. I love St. Paul's, the precious
chapel of Trinity Episcopal Church. The term chapel often
means small private spot. This is not small; it's huge with
forty-foot ceilings and elaborate Christian symbolism. The
huge pulpit, up about fifteen steps, is the very pulpit where
George Washington preached his inaugural address. Now
there is a massage table pushed up beside it.

St. Paul's Chapel is the oldest public building to be in
continuous use in Manhattan, and it was completed in 1776. So
many historic occasions in the life of our nation have taken

place in this chapel. I am privileged to be part of this the latest historic occasion.

My first assignment today was at the supply table, not the medical supply table, just the regular supply table. At first I thought I just wanted to be with the workers as they sat quietly, ate, or walked around reading. (After all, I am a Chaplain.) But I jumped right in and started organizing the table. (Dianne, I was organizing the table.) It was wonderful.

I took everything out of each green Tupperware bin, cleaned the bins and started over—sweaters, t-shirts and sweat shirts, yellow full-body rain suits, ponchos, blue or yellow, two-piece rain suits, gloves, work boots and rubber boots, hand warmers and foot warmers, face masks and replacements for the respirator face masks, scarves and knit hats, safety masks and shoe pads, orthodic shoe inserts, socks, socks, and more socks. (We really needed some of those hat covers that look like shower caps to put over the police regulation hats, but never have had any.)

I was in charge of passing out supplies for the needs of all the workers who came by. What a true pleasure. It started to rain. The construction workers were wet and grateful to get the yellow full-body rain suits. If they were too long, I just cut off the legs with scissors. The police can't wear yellow, and be regulation, so they got the blue ponchos. I put the blue ones in the back, under the table to save enough for them.

I hated the thought that they would be standing out in the rain for twelve or fourteen hours. With all of the clothing they already wear, they all needed help getting the raingear on. We needed more boots. One construction worker came in with soaking wet feet. He wore a size 7 $\frac{1}{2}$, but would have taken an 8 or 8$\frac{1}{2}$ with the extra socks. We didn't have any size 8 or 8$\frac{1}{2}$. The boots don't have to be new, just in decent shape.

I passed out rubber boots and lots of socks. They would sit down right there in a pew, take off wet socks and put on new ones. If theirs weren't wet, they would just put them on top of what they had on. Once again, I thought how much we are in this together. I would open boxes from behind the table and unpack the boxes or undo bags from Wal-Mart or K-Mart and other stores, putting things in the correct bins. It was wonderful to think about the love and generosity of a nation caring enough to send all of these supplies to make all the workers' lives more comfortable. I silently said a prayer for each person who sent the supplies I was opening. We opened case after case of blue ponchos, but ran out anyway. The stores of supplies upstairs are growing smaller.

I felt like a mother getting her children ready to go to the bus stop in the morning before school. We laughed and hugged and I would run to get them hot chocolate (I'm afraid my children would say this is better than I ever took care of them.) It has just occurred to me that I was the oldest person in the whole chapel that day or even in T-MORT . . . I might have been 20 years older than anyone else. One more blessing for me to be in this ministry is that I have always been grateful to play with my children's friends, and quite blessed to always be included with them, so I'm very comfortable with the Gen-Xers and don't even notice I'm not their age.

One worker came in and I, as usual, began chatting to him and asking him questions. No response. He motioned that he was going to eat. So he walked on. After he got his food I walked over to him and sat in the pew in front of him, turned around and asked him how he was, joking that I always ask a question as someone has just put a bite of lunch in his mouth. He looked at me with no response. He muttered something that sounded like "English."

"Oh," I said, "you don't speak English."

He didn't even understand that. But he knew that I knew . . . he speaks only Spanish. We began a complicated sign language/ body language conversation. I took out the tag from around his neck, which he had tucked into his overalls, and read that he was with Verizon. He was dirty, muddy, and so shy. Since I had seen the underground tunnels and huge three- or four-foot diameter Verizon conduits (maybe bigger, it's hard to estimate by looking down into the hole), I showed him that I knew what he did. He smiled and allowed me to get him coffee. Then I noticed he was wet. So I touched his shoulder and made rain motions he agreed he was wet. When I asked if he had a raincoat (good thing I took acting in High School!!!) with a shake of the head, he indicated, no.

While he finished his lunch, I went back to my supply table and got him a yellow poncho. Knowing he couldn't read any directions on the package, I just proceeded to take it out and to dress him. "Here you go, over your head. Hold up your arms; I'll hook the snaps." I told him he looked charming (he didn't have a clue). Gave him a smile and a quick hug. He only returned the smile and out the door he went. Imagine how lonely he must be all day not being able to talk to anyone. If he weren't so shy, he might try a few words. That poncho was a wonderful present for him.

Eight hundred thousand tons of debris has been removed since September 11. They found the radio tower today that was on top of the World Trade Center. Could they have said it was 300 feet tall? I don't think I heard that right, but they said huge. It was found in pieces, of course, but it was found.

Part of the time I was at the door, checking badges to make sure that only people with the appropriate credentials could come in. It seemed strange for me, "the queen of welcome and inclusion," to be turning people away from a church.

Later I showed two volunteers from a UCC church in Connecticut how to work the supply table and I began to move around the church to chat with the workers. Always the first answer they give me after being asked, "Hi, how are you doing?" Is. "Fine, how are you?" But then we begin to talk.

One very tall and bulky officer was sitting by himself on the far side of the church. I walked over; he gave me the flippant response, "Fine, what about you?" After a conversation that was as difficult as pulling teeth, he said he was mad with the whole world. Nothing could get worse. He worked September 11, lost several buddies, then had to work twelve on and twelve off for weeks, then his father died and his fiancé broke off the engagement and left. Times like that I feel so helpless; of course he was mad with the world . . . it didn't have anything to do with me. He wanted to be left alone to be angry. I was able to talk a moment about the stages of grief and that anger was one of them (yeah, yeah).

When I asked about his coping mechanisms he said, "Sometimes I drink, then other times I drink, but most of the time, I just drink."

"Hmmm, you feel pretty bad, don't you?"

"Yep, and it just can't get any worse."

I felt pretty desperate. What was I going to be able to do or say? Then he said, "I'm leaving tomorrow to go to Florida for a week. I'll get out of this hell hole and be with family for a week."

Asking if I could get him anything, an abrupt, "No thanks." was his answer. There was so much pain in his life that there was nothing to laugh about nor even smile about. He was pretty upset and I was no help.

A highlight was seeing my two grappler operators again. They are the ones who were so very dirty they didn't want to shake my hand, and I told them how proud I was to shake their hand.

They both have very thick Italian accents and intersperse Italian words with English. When I saw them today they were just as dirty, but you would have thought we were sitting around a big Italian family Sunday dinner table. They each threw their filthy arms around me and gave me a kiss on each cheek. They were chattering so quickly I couldn't understand what all they were saying, but I was as glad to see them again as much as they were to see me. When I remembered that they drove the grapplers (I told them that at first I thought that they called them grabbers . . . all of us laughed) they were so pleased. Now that I have inside credentials, they want to take me out to the pit to show me their equipment. They are proud of what they do. So we made a date, my next trip to St. Paul's. I believe when you know people—any people and all people—well enough, you learn to love them. Our differences only add spice to life. My life is pretty spicy and I'm grateful.

A Pastor's Journal
Entry Thirty-One - NYC - Ground Zero
December 16, 2001

I look at the date I am writing and cannot believe that Christmas is nine days away and I have done nothing. However, the ministry I am doing here in New York IS my Christmas. Certainly it is a gift to me and others will just have to take it as such.

When I came up out of the subway last night there was a crowd gathered around the display windows at Bloomingdale's. I had to stop and take a look also, saying to myself, "Self, you didn't think those windows were that great before . . . so why are you going to stand with a big crowd to see them again?" The largest window on the end had four life-size (All of the windows displays are life size.) male singers, arranged in a snow scene, dressed in red tuxes with top hats. They looked as if they were standing just outside my living room window, preparing to sing Christmas Carols.

I love Christmas caroling and am always ready to go. All my life, I've been accustomed to caroling at nursing homes and in neighborhoods or at homes of shut-ins. When I first moved to Raleigh and went to a Christmas dinner party at a dear friend's house, we ended up singing around the piano. I begged everybody to go caroling in the neighborhood. The response was, "We don't do that here in Raleigh." Well, last year I convinced the same group to sing carols at least at one house and it was great fun.

In Manteo, a group of neighbors gets together every year to go caroling. It was only a few days after I had moved in when they came to my door. They were wonderful. Oh, not the music necessarily, although it was good, but the thought that they would come sing for me, someone they didn't even know, on Christmas Eve. Really, it was heartwarming. I loved all of the people in Manteo. What a great year—lots of smiles. I had a wonderful group of women friends for playing bridge, going antique shopping, and walking to the little movie theater a couple of blocks away. They took me in right away; I miss them.

Anyway, the window at Bloomingdale's was pretty, and I was about to walk on toward my hotel when suddenly the mannequins started singing! They were real people singing in the window just posing as mannequins. It was a serendipitous treat and made me really miss my Choraleer group in high school. We were a group of nine girls who would travel around singing. We were quite a crew (and good too!) at Christmas, dressed in our red velvet jumpers, white blouses and big ties. My high school music teacher, Louise Hopkins, was one of the greatest influences in my life. She believed in me, even though I marched to the beat of a different drum. I was an alto.

One of the sopranos, Suzie, is still one of my best friends; we went to dance class together when we were four or five. Being an Air Force brat, I moved a lot, so I don't have any other friends from grade school or high school. Suzie eventually performed on Broadway in some Andrew Lloyd Webber productions. I continue to be proud that I was her maid in each of our high school drama productions! Christmas always makes me nostalgic.

The commute to St. Paul's seems harder this trip. It doesn't take long to get out of shape physically. There are 26 steps to get from my hotel lobby down to the sidewalk level, 37 steps down to buy the subway ticket, 86 steps down further to catch the express, then fifteen more down at the Fulton Street Stop to go under the road and then back up on the other side. Coming back, I always think I'm going to die. Part of the climb is on a ramp and part on an escalator but the rest is stairs and the trek is just about killing me. Three months without aerobics will do it every time.

As soon as I entered St. Paul's, huffing and puffing, I saw the two men from the Department of Justice, with whom I had chatted a long time in November. They are really cool men with the Immigration and Naturalization Service. They are investigators and aren't allowed to talk about their work at all. One is from Texas and the other from Kansas City. They are part of a group of eight who came together and work for sixty days, never having seen each other before. They tell me that their work has been successful and that they will next go to Salt Lake City for the Olympics. We were very glad to see each other and we chatted for a while. I renewed acquaintances as well with the steelworker who had his car towed when President Bush arrived. It felt like old home week.

Beautiful music is wafting through the church. A woman is playing a medieval harp and singing tones (I learn later it's called Intuitive Improvisation Sound Healing.) Another woman is playing the flute, just following along I guess. It is gorgeous. The whole chapel, which is often full of frenetic people, with all that is going on, seems to take a deep breath, relax, and become more peaceful. I have never heard anything like it. Yesterday, the Vienna Boys' Choir sang in the chapel—I'm so sorry I missed that!

I spent some time with the massage therapist. She lives and works in this neighborhood, but her office was destroyed and she lost most of her clients. Now she volunteers here. Massage therapists seem to have their act pretty much together, understanding the relationship between body, mind, and spirit. I enjoy chatting with them. This therapist has worked on many celebrities, among them Martha Stewart (I don't remember who all she said). She was glad to tell her story.

I walked up to a tall thin man who was alone and eating. He had reddish-blond hair and a ruddy complexion. I introduced myself. With a huge grin, he introduced himself but the only word I understood of his introduction was "Ireland." Ah, but with slow repetition, I discovered that when he was in high school he had come to the Bronx from Ireland (no wonder I couldn't understand a word he was saying—what a combination!) He is older, cheerful, and had wonderfully funny, slightly bawdy, stories to tell.

He has a great outlook on life. His young partner joined us. Wouldn't you know it, he had pitch-black, thick, longer hair and was unshaven, shy, hunky, handsome, and filthy. They were as different as different could be. The younger man had a sweet smile. He took off a heavy tool belt and placed it in the pew. They are steelworkers, welders actually, with the construction crew. I do notice now that more and more of the workers are wearing their respirator masks. These two guys were great. We were chatting along (mostly the tall, thin one was chatting away) when the massage therapist came over to us and said, "I need a body for a massage." My eyes lit up.

"Not you." She quipped, and smiled. "I need a body for a photo shoot, one of the onsite workers."

I looked at my two and said, "Do it."

"No way," said the Irishman.

"Do it," I directed the younger one. "Matt, go do it."

"No, I've never had a massage."

"You'll love it and you'll be perfect."

"What do I have to do?"

"Come on, I'll go with you."

"Okay."

I stood beside him for thirty minutes while he got a massage and the TIME photographer took his picture from every angle. It will be in this year's last issue of TIME. He was so proud, and what a body he has to show off! The massage therapist was proud to be in the photos, too. Even I was proud for having talked him into it and staying with him. He thanked me, then put his shirt back on, hooked up his overalls, put on the tool belt and hard hat, and went back to Ground Zero. Was any ministry going on there?

I met two US Customs agents; one is from San Antonio, but it was the other one that I can't get out of my mind. They are here to remove the gold bullion and custom files from the building that had its front ripped off and was terribly damaged. He is staying with his family who live on the street where the flight from JFK to Santa Domingo crashed.

He is originally from the Rockaway neighborhood and his family is glad he's back here to work. Every day he rides in on the train to the WTC, then dig through the rubble looking for classified documents. On the morning of November 13, he was at home with his mother getting ready for his shift when the plane hit. It crashed right there on his street. It killed his neighbor and her son . . . they had been friends since high school. He seems numb and bitter. He's too young to be bitter. I'm not sure I was any help to him. He is definitely grieving, but isn't ready or willing to deal with it yet. He relayed a story about two who had made it out of the WTC just as it was collapsing. He told of how they had to run for their lives, covered in ash and debris but had made it, only to be on that plane flying to the Dominican Republic and be killed.

It is so very hard to understand. One of the most difficult lessons in this life is how unfair it is. It seems if we try to be good people, love one another, and live a life that is kind, then life should be kind in return. It just doesn't happen that way. Life is just what happens while we're making plans for something else. The key is how we handle whatever life brings us. Speaking as someone who has definitely NOT handled many life situations wonderfully, I can empathize with how terrible he feels in the midst of all of this unfairness.

We ended our conversation with his saying, "I'm just here doing my job; just doing my job."

When I asked if there was anything good in his life, he thought a moment and said, "I'll be with my family for Christmas . . . and they are all alive."

This Christmas of 2001, if we can say only that, we are truly blessed because there are thousands and thousands who can't. Camille, never forget how blessed you are. You will be home with your family for Christmas . . . and they are alive.

A Pastor's Journal
Entry Thirty-Two - NYC - Ground Zero
December 17, 2001

Last night I was talking to my mother on my cell phone as I walked to my hotel down 50th Street from the middle of Manhattan. The phone was in my pocketbook and I had the earpiece in my ear, so both hands were free. I was giving my mother a walking tour of New York. As I passed Rockefeller Center, I described the massive Christmas tree with its red, white, and blue lights, the ice skaters, the huge wreaths, the magnificent white lights everywhere, the enormous white star hanging at Tiffany's between the four high buildings at the corner of 5th Avenue and 57th Street, and the crowds filled with festive excitement. Mother couldn't believe that at almost midnight NYC was in full swing as if it were daytime.

I was chatting away, when a couple of guys passed going in the same direction, then turned around and looked at me as if I were crazy. They laughed. They must have thought I was enthusiastically talking away—descriptive hand motions and all—to no one. They could see I was alone but couldn't see the cell phone wire hanging from my ear. When they finally figured it out, they slowed, laughed more and started walking with me. Soon, three of their buddies caught up with us and we were all laughing about me, as I continued talking to my mother on my "hands free" cell phone. Well, Mother was practically hysterical with panic at my talking to strangers on the street at midnight in NYC . . . male strangers at that! But I could instantly tell they were fine. Well, almost instantly;

they took turns talking into my microphone, "Hi mom, we're firefighters from Texas, Reno Nevada (I forget where else)." Finally mother relaxed, since her brothers and all of our relatives had lived in Paris, Texas. She figures anyone from Texas has to be fine.

What drew the six of us together, really, was the terrorist attack. As we walked along, we shared our World Trade Center stories. They came up to participate in the memorial service yesterday and to pass out 15,000 audio CD's called "Angel" to the firefighters throughout NYC. The singer, Becky, from Texas, who performed the songs on the CD, also sang at the memorial service.

They said they drove 2,000 miles "code three" lights and sirens blaring to get here in time. We were instant comrades. (One of them sent me an e-mail today and said that in his 23 years of fire service, this experience was his most rewarding.) While I waited in the lobby of their hotel, they ran upstairs and got a CD to give me to bring home. I will cherish it. Their website is www.911angel.info It is a beautiful site and they are beautiful human beings. I only had seven more blocks to walk alone to get to my hotel. That was one more precious, serendipitous piece of good fortune.

It was thirty degrees when I walked to the train station this morning. I worked six hours at T-MORT and six hours at St. Paul's. It was really the first cold morning. If I had not been working, in the afternoon I would have gone to Trinity Church, which is just a few blocks from both sites. The Messiah was being performed there and I understand the sanctuary was packed. It was quite special this year since Trinity has been inside the barricade, in the Frozen Zone. Although not damaged, it was not used for two months. In 1770 Handel's Messiah made its United States debut at Trinity Church. How appropriate it is to it be performed once again at Trinity, as the dawn of a new era in American History (post September 11) is beginning.

I'm especially partial to this production because my brother, Jim Ogle, conductor of the Boise Philharmonic, has been coming to New Bern, North Carolina, the first weekend in December for 20 years to conduct the performance of "The Messiah." Not only is it a beautiful and inspiring event, but also I always have such a good time showing my pride in my little brother and being with him and his friends, who either sing in the choir or play in the orchestra. This year was no exception. Truly, Christmas is upon us and the New Year is right around the corner. The number "2" arrived today to be placed upon the top of #1 Times Square building so that when the ball drops on New Year's Eve, it will read 2002. Hard to believe . . . the last three months seem to have taken over the whole year of 2001.

The EMT firefighter lieutenant, as well as another of the EMT medics who were with me in T-MORT, had both been to the doctor yesterday for a physical. There is concern for their lungs and the possible effects of fallout from all of the chemicals and debris around the site. The young man was especially concerned that they took six vials of blood, "Why did they take six; why six? You know they don't need that much." When I asked about the results, they said the tests would take two months. They all agreed that they would probably be dead in ten years, or at least sick, because of this duty at the WTC site. What a sad thought for such young adults.

Two police officers sitting in the back pew got quite talkative after a slow start. They probably talked forty minutes. It seemed important to let them talk. I somehow don't think guys talk about this stuff among themselves. At least they act as if they don't. Maybe they're just too busy working. One of them was on the first bucket brigade while the other one worked in the first permanent morgue.

One of them spoke of how the site looks now, after they took down the last five-story piece of the WTC building yesterday; it was the North Tower, I think. Funny, I was just writing about that yesterday. He said it looks surreal, as if it should be the backdrop for the movie "Terminator" (which I never saw). The other chimed in, "Or maybe more like that Bruce Willis movie, 'Under Siege'." (I didn't see that one either but knew what they meant, nevertheless.)

They talked about a lot of gory things that I won't repeat. They acted as if they couldn't tell anyone else, but needed to tell me. They talked about jet fuel having splattered blocks away and molten temperatures melting parts of buildings and people. They told of firefighters and police, who had run in to get people, turned around to bring them out only to find that they couldn't get the doors open again. They called on their radios to say they had the people safe and were bringing them out but then couldn't get the doors open to get out. They didn't realize that the building had shifted because of the melting of the steel beams and the doorframes were askew and the doors jammed. Their friends and colleagues outside, tried to knock down the doors but had to run when the building was collapsing. Those inside were still screaming into their radios. Those outside still carry huge amounts of guilt.

One of the saddest events these two shared was that bodies falling from the top of the building had killed firefighters and police officers. The truth of this disaster is really much worse than anything Hollywood could make up.

The two officers are fearful for their families' mental health because they are gone all of the time working. They talked of exhaustion, yet they work out a little while every day to release stress. They feel that life will never go back to normal. I shared with them that this disaster is like a high school diploma. They won't take it out from under the bed to look at it often, but their lives will be changed by it forever. They agreed that they have already changed and know it will be forever.

The last of the memorial services was held today. Donovan was his name. How many days after, Ninety something? What pain these people have endured.

Earlier, I may have confused two stories. Now, as I think about it, the security guy had been hired by a special company to wait for the gold bullion, and it was the customs guys who were taking out files. I remember the security man because he was so very smart and had to just sit and wait in his car all day. He talked about how boring it was and how he had read every word of the newspaper several times. As he left I walked with him and gave him a stack of magazines (Boy, I wish that I could give him a few stacks of my magazines from home!) that were behind the supply table. I put them in a brown paper bag. He was overjoyed. It's the simplest things that can make someone happy!

I also remember that the man who could only speak Spanish said one word in Spanish that I understood. . . demolition. Maybe the word is Spanish. Too bad not one person has spoken any French—I could speak with them.

At one point we got slammed with people around dinnertime, so I grabbed a pair of gloves and started serving dinner. One of the serving volunteers said, "I've noticed how the workers all smile when they talk to you and how you smile with them. You have a wonderful easy smile. They all seem to leave happier than when they came in."

"Thanks," I said. "The smile was a gift. I guess I was just born with it." (Hmmm, maybe like my beautiful friend told me she was just born with her good looks.) My smile is a gift and I'm thankful for it. My name is too; I love my name.

I forgot to say that yesterday I rode in a cab and the driver looked just like Bin Laden—turban, beard, dress, coloring and everything. He seemed shy, more so than most. I believe he was saying prayers while he was driving (not about the traffic). I could see his head nodding gently and a low monotone came out as his lips gently moved. He was a very kind man and was quite appreciative of his tip. It must be hard for the Muslims in this country. They must all think that we hate them. I don't.

I saw one of the sanitation workers with whom I had spent time on several days in November. He saw my Red Cross Badge and told me he is angry with Red Cross.

"Not only did they steal all of that money, now they won't let sanitation workers in their respite center. Who do they think was here first working 24 hours a day beside the police and firefighters? The sanitation workers, that's who. Who do they think cleans all of the toxic debris away? We do."

He was here yesterday and said, "I'm surprised they didn't use a firefighter for that TIME magazine thing. The whole world forgets how many of us are working twelve- to fifteen-hour days around the clock day after day. The firefighters get all of the press, all of the glory." He seems so angry and so tired.

I remembered where he lives and said, "How is Stanton Island?"

"How should I know? I only sleep there and don't do much of that. I don't have a life anymore."

I had to leave him to read the scripture in the twelve o'clock mass. No one listened and I noticed he was asleep. Good for him, he needs the sleep more. I read from a translation of the Bible that even I don't understand—NOBODY listens. Makes me question a lot! Later, when he was getting ready to leave, I took him by the arm to a "special stash of homemade cookies" and I got two for him. He smiled for the first time. I put my finger up to my lips, as if a secret. He nodded, his lip quivered and he walked out. Oh my God, if I make any difference at all . . . it is so small . . . so very small.

A Pastor's Journal
Entry Thirty-Three - NYC - Ground Zero
December 18, 2001

The workers are really tired and quite frustrated by their schedules. This is my third trip to ground zero and we are more than ninety days into the clean-up effort; people are exhausted. They are tired of it—period. Tears are much closer to the surface. Frustration is apparent. It is tougher now because this season, even under normal circumstances, brings people the "holiday blues". Somehow we have a glorified picture of what families should be like, look like, and act like. That picture is usually just a fairy tale.

It seems all the holiday movies portray the miracle of people falling in love and receiving exactly, and unbelievably, what they want for Christmas—happy Tiny-Tim endings. Most lives are not fairy tales. We have visions of beautiful people in beautiful clothing, kissing other beautiful people at beautiful parties, receiving beautiful gifts at beautiful holiday events. For the majority of Americans this, too, is just a dream, not reality.

Expectations are nearly always too high. We expect our family members and loved ones to act differently from how they always do and then we are disappointed that they act the same during the holiday season as they always do. We spend too much, eat too much, drink too much, sleep too little, and then wonder why we don't feel so great; all when the media says we SHOULD feel wonderfully joyful during the holiday season.

It's no wonder the workers' tears are so close to the surface when you add all that to the seasonal depression, perhaps caused by light deprivation. After all Friday, December 21 is the shortest day of the year. Then add the stress, strain, fear, fatigue, and anxiety of the terrorist attacks of September 11; add to that the fact that the country is at war and these workers at the World Trade Center are working—twelve hours on, twelve off—six or seven days a week. It's no wonder they are depressed, angry, and hurting.

As I look at the intense pain in the eyes of those around St. Paul's I feel frustrated . . . how can I ever hope to make even a tiny dent in the profound sadness in their worlds? The stress and strain of the extra grueling work is definitely disturbing their mental and emotional health. Thank goodness I come to New York for a short time and then have an opportunity to go home and regroup.

Even though my room is "the Ritz," this trip, I'm having more trouble sleeping. For the third night, I only slept four hours. Maybe it's my working in T-MORT. Maybe it's my sadness at the fact that, because of financial limitations, I might be able to make only one more trip up here. I hope I can come back early in January. Both the Red Cross and Sister Grace, at St. Paul's, are encouraging me to set my schedule now.

I took a cab home from the site last night because I had something too heavy to carry on the train. The cabbie told me he is a writer and an actor and I believed him instantly. He noticed my hard hat and asked what type of work I was doing at the site. I told him and then he told me his story of September 11. He was in his cab, parked in front of the Marriott, immediately to the west of the WTC and heard the explosion and saw pieces of building falling. He remembered the earlier bombing of WTC and thought that this time it must have happened at the top. He wasn't really afraid of dying but, with everything falling, he just was sure something would come crashing through the cab and impale him. He then saw bodies falling and was so confused and disoriented that he didn't know which way to go.

He started driving and after a few blocks saw the second plane hit, not knowing that the first explosion had been a plane crash also. Traffic was so bogged down because of the wailing of the emergency vehicles' horns that he was stuck in the bumper-to-bumper traffic and actually saw the collapse of both buildings. The confusion and panic he witnessed will be forever burned into his memory.

He too is suffering, but he seems to have a good spiritual life and appears to be taking care of himself. He is such a gentle soul; softly, he was playing a CD of holiday music. He told me the music seems to calm the people he picks up and make them happier. He believes that all of New York City is suffering. He said the people are generally depressed and not moving around the city as much. We exchanged e-mail addresses. How will I ever get these people out of my mind . . . and heart?

Today, I had two interesting theological discussions with two different people. Hmmm, both of their names were the same.

The first had been a port authority police officer and then got a master's degree in engineering while still working at the Port. He is supervising the structural work on the buildings that are to be saved as well as helping the construction workers with matters of safety underground. He is a very strict practicing Catholic, has two young children, and comes into St. Paul's every day to light a candle, sit in the back, and listen to the mass. (OK, so I have to eat my words about no one listening.) He is very comforted by the liturgy. I like him a lot and he wanted very much to talk. He's the first person I've met in three months who claims an active church life. Wow.

The Port Authority Offices were in the World Trade Center. So he had worked there for years and knew everyone. Fifteen of his best friends were killed and one made it out alive. He said that many were talking on their cell phones while the tower was collapsing; they were describing the sound of the collapse to be like that of a train about to run over them. Their spouses heard the noise, all of the screaming, and were still talking to them as they were crushed and died. One of his friends called his wife at home to tell her he was about to die in the tower as it was crashing down. She was not at home and he left the message on her voice mail. She listens to the message over and over. His voice and the sounds in the background haunt her. This beautiful Catholic man takes care of himself by getting up at four a.m. every day and riding his bicycle, looking at the skyline as it now is and thinking about what it was. He says he cries alone each morning and prays for his dead friends as he rides. He hopes that having his own two young children in Catholic School will protect them from some of the pain the city, country, and world is feeling. It would be nice to think that we could somehow protect our children. If only it were possible.

Liberty Island is going to reopen on Thursday, for the first time since September 11, but for security reasons, the Statue of Liberty will be closed to the public indefinitely. Its closing reminds me of how we must make the most of each day—take every opportunity, every little moment of joy that comes our way because there is no promise of a tomorrow. I know how good chocolate tastes, but the moment before I eat it the anticipation is almost as good, and certainly, the memory is good as well. If I appreciate only the highest points of life, I miss much of the everyday joys. It's as if I have "Statues of Liberty" in my life constantly, but I fail to climb them. I want to taste every moment, savor every smell, climb every Statue of Liberty; for this is the only moment I am given.

Crime is down in NYC since September 11, pretty amazing since in other large cities across the US, crime is up. Here there is a renewed sense of ownership and pride . . . powerful!

I'm not allowed to wear my Red Cross badge inside of St. Paul's. It seems that there is a controversy between the Red Cross workers and those at St. Paul's. I try not to mention one when talking to the other. It's too bad, but it happens.

I spoke with the tall, thin Irish man again. I love his spirit. I asked about his young partner, Matt.

With a quick smile and wit he replied, "Oh, the TIME magazine model? He's so famous he must have celebrated too much last night and didn't make it to work today." He said, "Chaplain, come out here and wait for me. I made you something but I have to do one thing to finish it."

I waited outside the construction barricade. In a few moments he came back with something in a piece of burlap. I couldn't imagine . . . it was smoking. When he opened the burlap, there was a huge, gorgeous Celtic cross he had made for me out of a steel I-beam. I couldn't believe it. Oh yes, he is a steelworker . . . a welder. It is the most beautiful present I have ever received. It weighs 20 pounds but feels like a hundred. Why did he do this for me? Of all of the people I have spent time with I never would have thought . . .. I normally have a huge problem receiving gifts but this one makes me overjoyed.

Christmas is a time of gift-giving. I'm not usually good with gifts, neither giving nor receiving. I think it has to do with motive. The gift from the Irish steelworker has no strings attached—period. The gift was not required, nor was it expected. It wasn't even the correct date to give it. It did not have to be wrapped a certain way, nor was I expected to respond with ooos and ahhhhhs. He did not make it for me out of shame or guilt or obligation. It was a pure gift of himself. I love it. Gift-giving can be an addiction for many people and Christmas just intensifies that problem. It can be just like alcohol, as it at first brings a sense of well-being and pleasure. It enhances self-esteem, but that feeling goes away soon and more must be given to reclaim the same result. The cycle can soon become uncontrollable and obsessive, and thinking about it can even interrupt daily living. More people file for bankruptcy in the first of the year than any other time, because unbridled spending has left them deep in debt. I wish I could have a healthier, more balanced sense of gift-giving, rather than just not wanting to participate in the process at all. It is really sad for me to just want that part of Christmas to be over as soon as possible.

The other theological conversation was with a man who is a construction worker, doing demolition on the site. He asked if we could talk theology.

Uh-oh, I don't usually do that here. "Sure," I said, "what's on your mind?"

"I don't celebrate Christmas . . . the Bible says not to."

He began to quote scripture. At first I thought maybe he just felt the same as I do about our overabundance of things and his attitude had to do with the commercialism of the spiritual holiday. No, he was a biblical literalist. He had read his Bible cover to cover four times and had it on tape to listen to in his car. I had to really think about what I said to him. Camille, remember to be an instrument of God, you must be able to converse in their language. Wow, God do I really have to do this?

He talked much of the devil, hell, three resurrections, end times, the splitting of the curtain when Jesus died, feast of the tabernacles, and things I hadn't thought about since Divinity School. Theologically, we are 180 degrees apart, but personally I like him a lot. He had been raised Catholic then had rebelled and became Holiness Pentecostal, rebelled again, and became his own self-taught authority without a community. I prayed the whole time we were talking that I would not offend him and that I could hear his real issues. Mostly, I nodded and let him talk.

He kept saying, "Thank you so much for this conversation, I just needed to talk about this."

He talked on about the devil calling Bin Laden and the fires of hell falling out of the building. He quoted Isaiah, Revelation, and Exodus; he talked about the perfect creation in Genesis. I listened.

Finally I had the courage to say, "Tell me about the most painful part of your life since September 11." Well, we were bosom buddies by then and he just put his head down on the pew and began to weep. He believes his life to be a mess and wishes he had been one of those killed so he could be called a hero. I cried with him. I was attracted to him, in spite of his theology. He was handsome, very bright, quite enthusiastic and charismatic . . . also 51 years old (looked younger). Probably the oldest person I have met up here.

As his story unfolded, we never again mentioned theology; he shared a lifetime of pain. He had not gotten married until 1988 when he was 38. He was alone when his father died in '84; then his fifteen-year-old dog died in 1985. He cried even harder when he told me about her. She was like his child, then his mother died in '86. The losses were so painful for him. As he spoke, the vocalist sang "Ave Maria" with the most gorgeous piano accompaniment. I thought I was going to sob my own heart out. I had to get napkins for both of us.

He had started college but got bored, dropped out, opened his own construction company, and his father was never proud of him. He married in '88, but in a few years his wife began having an affair and ran off with another man. It broke his heart. I understood and wept with him. He wasn't divorced until the mid-nineties because he fought it so hard. I understood. I told him he must have been so humiliated and felt like such a failure. He nodded. I said you must have felt so alone and been so embarrassed. He nodded and cried. My nose, too, was running, as a violin joined the music. He said the only thing that keeps him going is his Bible.

Wow. Oh, my what a story. How could I help? He said I had helped by just listening. The World Trade Center attack had confirmed for him that the devil was loose in the world. The pain and sadness of the attack and those lost souls (who he did not believe were with God) had just made his life worse. We talked of his years of pain and of the cumulative affect of the WTC attacks. I taught him how to journal the Psalms, as Father Murphy had taught me to do at Duke my first year of

Divinity School. He liked that plan and agreed to do it. I told him that the laments would be especially helpful. He liked that idea a lot. (We were pulling ourselves back together.) I then taught him how to pray a scripture, by becoming one of the characters in the story and feeling it, as Father Westerholf had taught me in my second year of Divinity School. He thought that was really cool and promised to try. We left with hugs and after he got all of his gear back on, he came back over to shake my hand and said he couldn't wait to share all of this with his girlfriend back home.

There were three African-American policewomen talking together, just girl talk. I asked if I could join them. Soon we were talking about all of us being women in men's jobs. We all concluded that we need wives to make our lives easier and laughed. They fussed about still having to do most of the work at home . . . or it just wouldn't get done. They talked about their children and about having no time to get ready for Christmas.

I told them it was great to spend a few minutes with women. We bonded. Two of them had their feet up in the pews and were hoping that the podiatrist was there to give them shots in their feet. Standing for twelve to fourteen hours a day, six days a week, was killing them. They probably wear ten to fifteen pounds of gear and all three fussed about gaining fifteen pounds since September 11. They said it was from all the free food everywhere and every volunteer wanting to feed them. They admitted that they ate just to make everyone feel better, and eating helped alleviate their stress.

They joked that there was no way they could run after a suspect with all that they had on and the way their feet felt. The podiatrist wasn't there, so I went over to the supply table and got magnetized shoe inserts. At first they didn't want me to bother with their feet, but soon I was cutting the inserts to fit their shoes and massaging their feet before they put their shoes back on. It felt holy . . . a little bit like ministry.

A Pastor's Journal
Entry Thirty-Four - NYC - Ground Zero
December 19, 2001

The estimated number of those killed in the terrorist attack at the WTC is down now from 6,000 to 3,000. That is still terrible, but not so terrible. One of the firefighters told me about his going home from the Airplane crash on November 13 and sitting down with his wife at the dinner table that night. He told his wife he was worried about his feelings.

He said, "Honey, I just pulled 255 dead, burned bodies from the crash in Rockaway today and, after working at the WTC, it didn't even affect me. It felt like it was just all in a day's work."

He told me that any other time the crash would have been one of the worst disasters in America and that he just took it with a grain of salt.

He said, "I don't feel anything. Am I heartless?"

He and I talked about self-protection mechanisms and about denial and shock. We talked about what to watch for in the future—symptoms of post traumatic stress syndrome. We talked about feeling numb. I need to watch for that myself! What an awful experience this has been for these young workers.

The school in Tribecka is not going to open as planned in January. Evidently, the air is not clean enough to be safe for the children to breathe. The school is just a few blocks from the World Trade Center site. Yesterday there was a fire at St. John's the Divine. It was a five-alarm fire, and I heard about it from a firefighter who had been listening to his radio inside of St. Paul's early in the morning. St. John's is the world's largest Gothic cathedral. It was there I got my Red Cross Certification in November. I understand that two priceless seventeenth-century tapestries were damaged. Their thirty-services-a-week schedule is on hold for the time being, due mostly to water and smoke damage. I pray that their services can be held elsewhere for Christmas and will resume at St. John's soon.

My schedule this time is terrible. I made it myself—Did I think I was a superwoman or something? It's not easy to find time to journal. Working at night and then alternating during the day, I'm finding it very difficult to have the time and energy to sit down and stay focused. Just the scheduling feels overwhelming.

It's a good thing that we all work together as a team while we each just do our own little part. The more I know of the ever-expanding rippling effects of the collapse of the towers and see how great and far-reaching the impacts are, the more my ministry seems so insignificant.

One of the high-ranking officers in the fire department had a meltdown when he was with me in the middle of the night.

He is totally exhausted. The meltdown started when someone called him and said they had tried to call him but he didn't answer his radio and they listed him as "no response." Evidently, being "no-response" is a huge faux pas, because he went ballistic at the caller. (I'm sure in his former life he was a sailor!)

Interspersed with graphic language was his assessment that, sitting in an office building, they didn't have a clue what it was like at Ground Zero. He yelled, "Sometimes the radios don't even work in the pit, and I'm 'bustin' it' doing what is necessary."

When he was through with the caller, he had his meltdown as he related the difficulties and impossibilities of his job. No one really has a clue about the scope of this situation. It is 27 acres of rubble, debris, bodies, ash, mud, etc. Think about it, twenty-seven acres. A football field is less than one acre. This project is huge. This kind and sensitive fire fighter was experiencing an overwhelming feeling that his little part didn't make any difference anyway . . . then someone put him down for the work he WAS doing . . . it was devastating. It's hard to tell the difference between grief and rage, especially when anger is such a necessary part of the grief process. Where do we put all of this anger?

One Bronx police officer says he and seven others made it to the site in twelve minutes. He's proud of his colleagues and said that more Bronx officers died in the towers than Manhattan officers.

He said, "We are the toughest and bravest." But he was sad as he told me. He said before the towers fell, his mother called. She was worried about him.

He told her, "No mom, I'm still in the Bronx, don't worry."

He asked, "Chaplain, it was ok for me to lie to her, don't you think? Boy, it's a good thing I got out. She would have been so mad if I had lied to her AND died." He smiled at the thought of it. I did too. That was the last in our conversation that we smiled.

He told his story—As his friends went rushing in he heard the voice of God saying, "The building's going down . . . get out." It was the first time ever he had run away from a disaster, and he felt terribly guilty. He believes his life was spared for some reason. As he ran, the building began to topple. He was hit with debris and only turned around once to see the smoke billowing from the top and the sky grew dark and he knew it was coming down.

He asked, "Do you believe I really heard the voice of God?"

"Yes, I do. (He is younger than my youngest child.) It was not your time to die."

"But I feel guilty. Those were my buddies from the Bronx who died. But I didn't. They were tougher and braver than I was."

"Yes, you feel guilty but for some reason you heard a voice telling you not to go in at that time. Now as you work through your pain and your guilt, listen for the voice again (Samuel) to answer your question of where to go from here. Be patient. Let yourself grieve."

Later in the day, he came in and said across several rows or pews, "Hey, Chaplain, you want to adopt me?"

"Sure, Honey." I replied. "Will you fit in my suitcase?" Oh, they are so young to be facing such pain.

In T-MORT, at the end of a shift, a lieutenant came in to replace the officer in charge. He said, "Hi Lieutenant, was it a good night? Did they recover many bodies on your shift?"

Very soberly, she replied, "Yes, I logged in about fifteen; but no, it was a terrible night."

His head tilted, questioningly. She continued, "They have not found my partner yet, nor any of his gear."

I had been with her all night, and we had talked about a lot of things, but she had not told me that one of the two medics who was lost was her friend, or that she kept wanting to find something of him. I think twelve EMTs in all were lost.

She said, "We found an identifiable ax but nothing from the medics."

She had told me earlier that she knew she needed counseling. She said T-MORT was really getting to her but that no one could understand, no one. The book of details, which she called "the book of horrors," was more than she could take any more . . . she was the one writing the details while I read from the tags. Bless her heart. No one should have to go through this inhumane disaster. I really feel helpless.

I often have mixed emotions about Ground Zero—death, yet opportunities for new life. Well, that happened again last night. It happened BIG TIME when I told the group I was working with, in T-MORT, about the flag. I had brought the North Carolina flag to be placed on the top of one of the cranes. The man who ran the crane had asked for it. Dan Gearino, a features columnist from the Raleigh News and Observer, had called the Governor's office and got a flag that had flown over the Capital. I went with a friend from CIC to pick it up, and then I brought it to NY.

The captain in T-MORT spoke up, "I'll take you in there. What color is your pass?" I held up my pass. "Green, Full Access," he said. "Great, get the flag, let's go."

As we walked out, the lieutenant handed him her camera and said, "If you can get a picture of her giving it to him, do it."

We went out and climbed into the "Gator" (I accidentally called it a cricket . . . they laughed at me.) The Gator is an all-terrain vehicle whose six wheels go up and down independently and it goes over rough ground like a snake. It's the only thing that can be driven into the pit (besides the big construction equipment). With hardhats and respirators, we went further into Ground Zero than I had been before. We drove down the hill where they are working four stories below ground, only to discover that the largest crane had been shut down the day before. They were disassembling and sending it to another site.

The captain said, "Don't worry, we'll fly it from another crane."

We drove all around asking questions. Finally we ended up at one construction entrance, once again gated on the inside, surrounded by a fence covered with green burlap. Of all the good fortune, the police officer on duty at that interior gate was an officer with whom I had chatted earlier for a long time at St. Paul's. At that time he had a six-weeks-old baby at home (his first, a little girl) and he couldn't wait to start working nights again so he could spend time with his wife and baby during the day. (I don't think he sleeps much!). When we saw each other, we were elated. We hugged as if we were long lost friends; the Fire Captain was likely surprised. We got right in, of course, and found the proper place.

We posed for a picture. Standing right at the edge of the hole is the FDNY Captain, the NYPD officer, the young construction worker who will hang the flag, the crane operator (a different crane . . . and on the night shift) and me, all standing behind the flag holding on to it. I am truly grateful to each of them for making it happen; all of us were proud to be doing it.

There we stood, grinning, proud that the mission had been accomplished and North Carolina would have one of the few state flags flying over the WTC site. I was so proud to be standing with these men who were actually doing the work. They were proud of themselves at that moment as well.

Then came my dilemma. In the background is the rubble of the worst disaster in American history. In the background are the remains of thousands of human beings still not recovered. In the background are billions and billions of dollars of destruction. In the background are the remnants of millions of affected or destroyed lives . . . and we are smiling proudly.

What should I do? Destroy the four pictures? Take away the credit and memory of what those who are working at Ground Zero are doing, stop life because of death? Is it sacrilegious to be smiling and standing on the ash pile of the WTC? It seems that when I studied ethics, decisions weren't that difficult. I thought then that being a basically good person, I would know the answer to these kinds of questions. This truly is an ethical problem for me! This is horrible ground but also holy ground. It signifies death, but it also signifies new life bursting forth from the tomb. How would a wife, or mother, or a child of one of the 3,000 killed feel if they saw my big grin as I so proudly held my state flag in my hands? How would they feel seeing the rubble so close to my heels, their pain so near to my fingertips? Oh, dear, God, why are the decisions in real life so complicated?

After my shift, I began to walk toward the train station in the darkness. I was just sort of shuffling along, with mixed emotions about the site and the state flag. When I looked outside of the barricades, I saw the Christmas decorations once again. On the top of every light pole throughout the financial district, there is a white star with streamers behind, a shooting star—a light in the darkness. The joyous decorations are a stark contrast to the site itself and to the hundreds of mourners still standing at the gates. I bet the city had ethical questions about whether or not to hang those decorations at Ground Zero. Real life decisions are so difficult.

A Pastor's Journal
Entry Thirty-Five - NYC - Ground Zero
December 20, 2001

What a beautiful day to wake up in New York City! The rain has moved out and there are no clouds in sight. Outside my window the sunrise is beautiful. Up Lexington Avenue, beyond the buildings, the sky is dark blue with cottony puffs of pink. The car lights still stream southward and the Christmas lights are still quite visible in the dim dusky light. I have already run down and bought a banana at the market just four doors away. I took all of my pills with the banana. Also at the market I got a small carton of orange juice to use in making my green super food. I did stop at Starbucks on the way back for an iced decaf mocha . . . just as a treat, and because I deserve it. Deserve it or not, I wanted it. It is yummy. Rachel's friend Uk made me my first one. Just one more thing I love . . . oh well.

WRAL, one of the North Carolina TV stations, is coming to my room this morning. I always think I won't have one intelligent word to say, and of course my hair will look terrible. I will ask them if they can make me look thin and young—they'll laugh their heads off.

Last trip, I asked the reporter to make me look young and thin. He said, "Camille, I'd be glad to do that but I'd lose my job." He laughed, then added, "No touch-ups allowed." So, newspapers and TV do sometimes reflect reality. My looks, what a stupid thing for me to worry about.

Yesterday I had a debriefing session (counseling) with another of the chaplains, one I've known since October. We had talked one day and he said he was a little concerned about me, since I had heard and seen so much at Ground Zero. He offered me a session and I jumped at the chance. Yesterday, on the telephone, I said to Jack Duckworth, my Webmaster, "If you don't ever hear from me again it will be because the counselor has me locked up." We laughed.

The counselor didn't have me locked up. Our session was enlightening. We agreed that I don't internalize any emotions—what I feel just comes out: tears, sadness, anger, fear, whatever—in this situation, that is very healthy! We agreed that I'm not a likely candidate for post-traumatic stress syndrome but that I'll need to watch for the symptoms for the next year or so. We also agreed that my motive is pure and it certainly is easy for me to do what I do. All of my gifts, talents, education, and experiences have brought me to this place at this time in my life to serve others. God's call comes at the intersection of human ability and human need.

However, not all that glitters is gold. When he asked about my personal life in Raleigh, my response sounded a bit bleak, especially the absence of an intimate personal relationship. His take on my ministry at Ground Zero was that it enabled me to keep my own life on hold. He's right. He said that I have about 25 intimate relationships a day at Ground Zero, so I wouldn't even notice that my own life is lacking. I had to agree. I hate it when counselors peg me!!!! He suggested that I evaluate how many more times I should come as a volunteer at Ground Zero. He said not that I don't do a great job and not that my ministry is not needed, but the longer I continue to come to NYC the longer I put off having to face my own life. Rats, I didn't want to hear that!!!

Lately, I've thought that I would like to spend Christmas right here in NYC. Being inside St. Paul's feels like being with family, a huge family. Many of the workers will continue to work right through Christmas. Oh well, I know about that. When you're a pastor you work until Christmas morning every year, with the midnight candlelight service. And if Christmas falls on a Sunday, well . . . but this year I will go home for Christmas. My children and mother would kill me if I stayed up here.

A police officer was sitting quietly, alone. He was tall, thin, handsome, and appeared a little withdrawn. However, when I began talking with him, he was friendly and open. He told me that, as of today, 479 rescue workers died in the terrorist attack.

He said, "It nearly was 480."

I said, "Go on."

He said that this is his precinct, so he was actually standing right below the WTC when the first plane hit. Looking up at the buildings, he couldn't tell what had happened, but when he saw the fire, he knew the sprinkler system had failed or been destroyed. He ran in and began yelling for people to get out.

His radio was going crazy with information, commands, and confusion. Pretty much the next few minutes were a blur. He stayed, ran in, and was getting people out. At the end he was carrying a woman who had fallen down the stairs while hurrying out. Debris, airplane tires, and people were falling. He really didn't know what was happening. When the collapse began, he was outside and so many of his friends were inside. They yelled at him to open the door, but he couldn't and they couldn't. The building had shifted and the door had jammed. A piece of building or debris of some kind fell on him. He got up and ran as far as he could then dove under a car, tearing up both his knees. EMT's found him under the car and he remembered only diving under the car and then waking up in an ambulance bandaged and dazed.

He asked the EMT's what had happened and when they told him and said they were taking him to St. Joseph's hospital, he screamed at them to let him out. He said there were others who needed their service. He got out of the ambulance and ran back. The next sixteen hours were a blur to him and most he doesn't remember. He spent the next day in the hospital. He had a concussion, severe abrasions, and was suffering from smoke inhalation.

When I asked him about his feelings now, he said he could still hear the voices of his friends inside the building. He knows he did his best, working harder than even he believed he was capable of, but the vision of his friends being alive, yet trapped, haunts him daily.

I asked him how he is doing emotionally now and he said, "My life is the pits and I'm just going through the motions." His divorce became final the first week in September. My heart ached for him. His wife had been having an affair. We talked about the humiliation and embarrassment (after all, he is NYPD!).

He said, "It's worse than that—she left me for another woman."

He is really hurting. I found no words of wisdom for him, but he still thanked me for eating lunch with him.

He said, "With all of the crowds around Ground Zero, I am still so lonely. Thanks just for talking to me. It's nice to have company for lunch."

As I walked away from him, I felt so helpless. Life is so very difficult for some and I fuss about wanting to look younger and thinner. Get a grip, Camille. Real life is difficult, but God is present in the form of hope, and in real relationships of listening and love, yes, mostly LOVE!

I had hung a T-shirt, which had been made by one of the children at Grace Community Church, on George Washington's pew inside St. Paul's. It's nice to see something from Raleigh, hanging right there every day.

There were two adorable policewomen who were sitting alone near the front far side of St. Paul's. I went up to them and we talked. They had great attitudes. The blond was hysterically funny even though she was terribly stressed. She obviously uses humor to diffuse her horrible feelings. They had been two blocks away, at Governor's Plaza, when the first plane hit. Their worst memory is that of hearing the beeping of the radios of their colleagues, inside the huge pile of debris, but not being able to get to them. They said it was so loud that is sounded like a group of birds chirping.

The blond spoke of the problems of having three children at home. The oldest, a boy, is her stepson who had just come to live with them on September 10. She said her life is so miserable that she doesn't know which is worse, being at work or at home. It was raining and they had on a ton of clothing. She said on top of everything else, her neck was killing her.

I said, "Go over to the chiropractor. I've been chatting with him all day. He is volunteering from New Jersey and is a really great guy. "

She thought about it and I could see the wheels turning. "Oh I have to take off all of this stuff and . . ."

"I'll help you with the stuff and tell him to wait for you."

"Ok," she said. Off with the blue poncho, the police coat, the gun belt, the bulletproof vest and over to the chiropractor.

While she was gone, the other one said that it would be good for her because her neck had been hurting for a week. It wasn't four minutes before the blond was back with a big smile.

I said, "How was it?"

She got right in my face, opened her eyes really big and with a huge smile said, "Orgasmic! Watch my stuff. I'm going outside to have a cigarette."

We all hooted. Then she said, "Maybe I shouldn't have told that to the chaplain." She turned to me saying, "You might want to run over there and get your neck adjusted."

We three roared with laughter. The rest of the day, as they would come in for breaks, the blond would give me the thumbs up and mouth the words "thank you."

Yes, in the middle of the rubble and the horror of Ground Zero, life goes on . . . and some of it is even good.

A Pastor's Journal
Entry Thirty-Six - NYC - Ground Zero
December 21, 2001

I got a call from the young man who had worked on floor 104 WTC, but had been on vacation when the towers collapsed. All of his friends had died in the collapse.

He said, "Have you walked into any of the stores since you have been here?"

"No, I replied, not one."

"Good, I haven't either. Will you meet me at the North West corner of Madison and 60th at five p.m. and shop with me?"

"Of course I will."

We met and walked up to Central Park on Madison, going into every store. He bought a few small things as Christmas presents. Then we crossed and came down 5th Avenue. He pointed out all of the private clubs and we visited many of the elite stores carrying specialty merchandise.

I had never in my life even been in to stores that had such huge price tags. I was way out of my league and felt like a hick, but at his side, at least an acceptable hick. It was good to listen to his conversation and see him laugh and smile. After 100 days of agonized grieving, he is definitely a little better. His girlfriend, who had gone back home to Brazil right after they returned from vacation, returned to New York for the first time this week. Her family would not let her come back to the United States. Her parents said it was too dangerous to be in the United States.

Wow, what a turnaround. Even he believes that life is so different after 9/11 that this relationship might not continue to work in the long-term, but he says it's good to have her with him now, especially during the holidays. I agree.

A counselor told me this young man would not truly be better until he begins to replace those friends he lost in the terrorist attack with new friends and starts a new life. From what I can tell, that has not happened yet. However, it was wonderful to see his transformation from our first two visits. Healing always takes place in baby steps.

We went to dinner and shared stories about our families. He felt encouraged that his business seems to be picking up again. I think he's beginning to see a tiny light at the end of the tunnel. However, he was very quiet and went home early. Healing is exhausting and it takes time to recover. It is hard work . . . period. I, on the other hand, wanted to stay out later. It was the only time this whole trip that I went out to dinner. I lost my beautiful black cashmere scarf. I must have left it in the cab. I hope it's not too cold before I go home.

It was a little challenging to work with a different medical examiner in T-MORT. He must have sensed my unease because after we had attended to three or four recoveries, blessings and prayers, he came back into T-MORT and said something like, "Hey whatever you need to do here is fine with me and however you want to do it is fine, just let me know. I sure don't want to upset the system or a chaplain and especially NOT God."

I laughed at the thought that he could offend God; he barely smiled. I said, "You're fine, don't worry, but it is important to me that I and all who wish to participate do the blessing in a certain atmosphere.

He said, "Sure, fine, I'll just try to be more sensitive."

It worked out and the rest of the shift went well. It was obvious that he was all business with the job to do (a very difficult job) and was like that Dragnet guy . . . "Just the facts ma'am, just the facts," or "Let's just get this job done."

I, too, needed to be more flexible and sensitive; not expecting that all ME's would work the same or feel the same about the chaplain's role.

I was serving coffee in St. Paul's while the beverage volunteer was on break. Two equipment workers in full gear, hardhats and all, and looking exactly like Mutt and Jeff came over. The white one about my height was pretending to beat up the other giant six-foot-six, 350-pound African American worker and said, "Don't give this big guy anything. No matter what he says, he really doesn't want anything to drink."

I played along. We joked together as the giant guy was ducking and bobbing, (dance like a butterfly, sting like a bee) pretending to be beaten up by the very small man. They got their cups of hot chocolate and moved away. The volunteer came back to her station and I moved into the sanctuary to chat. As I was talking to one man who wasn't really responsive, I noticed the giant man again sitting alone. He was about four rows back, in the very back corner of the last pew, a little hidden by the back pillar of the church. The big man made eye contact with me and smiled as he ate his dinner.

After finishing the conversation with the unresponsive man, I moved back four rows. The huge man was rather shy, considering his massive appearance. His appearance had convinced me that he wouldn't be needy in any way. Interesting how we make such instant assumptions based solely on looks. I consider myself not to be judgmental . . . yeah, right, Camille, it happens. I was wrong; this man NEEDED to talk to me.

He has been working a grappler at Ground Zero since September 12. He said he threw up when he found the first body and he went right to his supervisor and said he couldn't do it. His supervisor begged him to stay, "Just until they get things going."

He said he gagged and cried and couldn't stand to watch the dogs find bodies. The smell still kills him and he has nightmares. At first he begged daily to go to another job. He said it hurt him so much inside to put the grappler teeth into the pile and uncover any body parts. When he encountered body parts, he would have to get out of the cab and walk away while the next team did "their thing".

He commented on his own looks. "I know I look tough, but I'm not . . . I'm a wimp inside. I hate that about me."

I assured him that I understood how he was feeling anger at what he saw as a shortcoming, but also assured him that his disgust and revulsion showed that he was a human being with healthy sensitive feelings and . . ..

Before I could go on, he said, "That's not the end of my story. One morning before the sun had come up I was walking to my rig through the debris and it was gray and the air was thick with ash—you know it always depends on the humidity and the wind. For some reason it was still and quiet, or maybe that's just how I heard it that morning. Then a voice said to me, 'Thank you for what you are doing, you are doing it for me, for all of us that were killed. I know it is terrible job you have to do, but thank you for doing it . . . for us.'"

He said he still gags at the smell and says it is a smell he will never forget (I understand . . . all too well!) He still has a lump in his throat and tears up when he finds body parts, but every time he remembers that voice and thinks that maybe this is the one who spoke to him.

"So, I'm OK now, I still hate it, but I'll be here till we're finished. What do you think about that voice that came to me, do you think it is OK?"

Uh ooh, I need to respond. "Well, it's better than OK, but what do you think about the voice?"

"I think that it was the spirit of one of those in the WTC building, helping me get through this thing that is so hard for me."

"Yeah", I said. "Like maybe one of your angels."

"Yeah" he said, "like an angel, or like God or part of God."

"Yeah, I believe that we are all part of each other and all part of God."

I also affirmed his ability to hear the voice of God in the middle of that hellish war zone and to listen to it and pay attention. His eyes teared and he smiled such a sweet smile, then quickly said, "I'm late, I've got to go back to work, thanks for listening."

I never got to hug him or touch him even once. Poof, he was gone. "Samuel . . . Samuel, go back to bed and say, here I am."

It is cold outside now and the workers need many supplies, especially hand warmer packets, sweatshirts X-L, work gloves and navy-blue rain ponchos. Anyone wanting to send supplies to

Ground Zero may mail them to: St. Paul's Chapel, 209 Broadway, NY, NY 10007. Love letters can also be sent there.

A Pastor's Journal
Entry Thirty-Seven - NYC - Ground Zero
December 22, 2001

It was after dinner the dinner rush and he was sitting by himself on one of the chiropractic tables. The doctors and masseuses had long been gone for the day. I noticed the red, white, and blue bandana tied around his sandy-colored head, the strange angel earring hanging from one ear, and the ruddy young face. I didn't remember seeing him come into the chapel. It turned out that had been sleeping all day upstairs in the balcony on a cot. I went over and sat down beside him. His conversation was a bit too animated and his excuses prolific. He was a wonderful con artist.

It was only after I had gotten him dinner, new gloves, replacements for his respirator, new socks, and a sweatshirt to go under his coveralls (he was about to work the night shift), that I realized I was dealing with an addict of some kind. Nevertheless, I affirmed him in every way possible, especially his sense of call to Ground Zero to work.

He said, "I'm sleeping here at St. Paul's just for next couple of days, until I can get on my feet. I'm trying to stay out of the bars and off the streets."

Oh, homeless, I thought. Here he has everything but a shower, which was obvious!!! With a different set of volunteers everyday, he could charm the socks off unknowing folks everyday and hang out here a long time.

I spent a lot of time with him, looking at pictures he had taken and listening to his stories. It's beyond me how he managed to get his picture taken with every single celebrity that had come to visit ground zero! I gave him as much support as possible—one day at a time, one hour at a time, just one decision after another, calling on your higher power, recognizing you are powerless—the whole twelve-step bit. I hugged him and sent him out to work for the night, encouraging him to come get hot chocolate at each break.

After he left one of the staff of St. Paul's came up and said. "Was he sober?"

"Oh yes," I replied . . ."for the moment."

She shared, "When sober, you won't meet a nicer more polite young man, (con artist I thought) but when drunk, he is uncontrollably obnoxious. We have to put him back out on the street, three or four nights a week."

I wondered why I had never seen him before?

She continued, "Last week when he got paid (I don't want to be around on pay day!) it took five NYPD to even get him out of the church."

Yes, I could tell that he might be a problem, but this was my last time at St. Paul's for this trip. I'm going home for Christmas with mixed feelings, so I will never know how his night went.

Alcoholism is a difficult disease. There are probably many people who have tried to love him and nurture him in the past. I am sure there are people who have changed the locks on the doors and detached from him a million times. I have no delusions of grandeur to think that our interaction made any difference in his life whatsoever . . . in fact I probably just played his game, one more time. What is his answer? Is there an answer? Anyway, I don't expect to see him on my next trip to New York.

A middle-aged, stocky, overbearing, and rather unattractive police woman was standing alone in the back of the church to one side away from the supplies, food, beverages, and basically just standing alone eating something. It was not easy for me to go up to her. In fact contrary to popular belief, it is not easy for me to approach any of the people in St. Paul's. Every single time something from my own "stuff" gets in the way. I am always intimidated for one reason or another; usually it is the fear of rejection, but there are lots of other reasons. It is just that I do it anyway.

I walked up to her, silently, hoping she would just shoo me on my way gently. But no, immediately she started telling me her story—where she was on September 11 and how many days she had to work in this hell hole. She saw the buildings fall from John Street (where the oldest Methodist Church is). To her, the cries, screams, and the dark cloud and debris are as clear as if it were yesterday. She is very angry, more angry than most. She talked about her initial reaction not to panic—to see what she could do for those running, screaming and bleeding. I understood how she feels. In cases of emergency I go into my preacher mode, often jumping out of my car at an accident, or directing traffic for ambulances. Even after September 11, on planes, I'm sure that in the event of an emergency, I would not panic. I would attempt to calm those frightened. She did that too, on September 11, but feels a little bitter that she hadn't run home to protect those whom she really loves. I understood. It's a hard choice to make. Very often I feel guilty about choosing to respond where I respond. Nevertheless, she was so angry.

We were still standing and her story was just gushing, when she said, "My baby sister was living with me at the time and was dying with cancer." She started to cry and wipe her eyes with her napkin from the sandwich she was eating. "My baby sister died two days after the attack. Don't they know that her life is just as important as any one person who died in the WTC? Nobody cares about my baby sister. Nobody! Do her children get any love letters, or presents? NO! Are they included in the billions of dollars of aid for NYC? NO. And now I have her seven year old and 11 year old living with me and I just can't answer any of their questions." She tried hard not to sob, and so did I. "What should I tell them?" She asked.

I thought, "Oh, my God, does she really want me to answer? If I don't say anything maybe she will just keep talking. I don't know the answer. What should she tell them? Didn't I take a class in Divinity School that would give me the answer to questions like these? I don't know. I don't even remember what I told my own children when their daddy died and they were eight and eleven. Maybe I didn't tell them anything. Maybe we never talked about it enough. Maybe, I was so concerned with how terrible and lost I felt that I never even thought about them . . .. I don't remember."

She rambled on and I was not required to answer her question . . . thank God! "They need me at home, not here breathing in this toxic air and coming to work before they get up until they are almost ready to go to bed. I can't take it any more." Very loudly, she said again, "I can't take it any more!" Obviously, she was processing her own thoughts right in front of me. I was just like a sponge, nodding and crying with her, but not offering anything at all. Softly, she said again. "I just can't take it anymore."

She walked over to the garbage can tossed out the rest of her sandwich and garbage, turned around, took two steps back to me and said, "Thank you. I'm going outside now and tell the sergeant that I can't do this anymore. I have to be at home with my sister's children. I'm finished. This is it for me at Ground Zero. I'm out of here. Thank you."

As I watched her walk out of the church I was only slightly aware that I slowly shook my head, standing there wondering what had just happened. It was just a ministry of presence I guess. For truly, I did absolutely nothing, perhaps God did.

A Pastor's Journal
Entry Thirty-Eight - Raleigh, North Carolina
December 25, 2001

It's late in the evening on Christmas day and I'm at home in Raleigh.   All of the children and "adopted extras" have gone back to their homes. The kitchen is finally cleaned, with the second load of dishes running and a load of laundry going as well. The machine is filled with towels and tablecloths, napkins etc. Mother is asleep downstairs in the lounge chair beside the fire, in front of some TV Christmas special. My dog, Airlie is in her lap. It has been a long day but I feel great.

The nicest compliment today was to hear Rachel say, "I'm so glad you are the Kool-Aid mom, so we can always bring home our 'family-less' friends." But Julie and her family didn't get to come today; with a four-year-old and a twelve-year-old they decided to do Santa at home. Nevertheless, we talked to them several times during the day and there were still twelve of us for dinner.

At one point we were all sitting in the family room listening to Christmas CD's and waiting for the roast to be done. In blue jeans, sweat pants, or whatever, we were eating salmon, cream cheese with capers on toast tips, baked brie with brown sugar on crackers, homemade spinach dip, and enjoying a little holiday cheer when I asked Cris to check on the roast. She and Tyson were both in the kitchen.

Tyson opened the oven and Cris turned to him and said, "ooo Tyson, I just can't eat it that rare."

He came into the family room grinning from ear to ear. "Hey Mom, what time are we going to eat?"

"In about fifteen minutes or so."

"Good," he said still grinning, "what time do you want to turn on the oven?"

Oh, no. Well, it's a good thing we had a lot of hors d'oeuvres and a lot of holiday cheer. Two hours later we ate—so much for the perfect Christmas dinner.

Right as we were getting ready to say the blessing, the doorbell rang and we had two more for dinner. We quickly got another table and cloth, pushed it up to the already-set Christmas dinner table and there was plenty for all. The funny thing was, I only knew one of the new arrivals and no one said anything to me about who the other was.

After dinner and dessert and we cleared the dishes, we were once again all listening to Christmas CD's (new ones that one of my website-journal readers had burned herself and sent) in the family room when the surprise guest started talking about her son. I then realized she was the mother of one of the men already there. What a hoot. None of them could believe that I wasn't in on the conversation or the telephone call to invite her to come to dinner (hmmm, I must have been in the kitchen trying to make the roast cook faster!!!). All during dinner, she sat beside me and we chatted, and I didn't even know who she was. It was too funny but perfect to illustrate how I believe Christmas means . . . room for all, always, no questions asked, period.

Evidently, I have some strange ideas about Christmas. I love to ask the question of people, "exactly where in the Bible do we find the whole nativity scene, the one with angels, and shepherds, and wise men and stable and all?" Of course the answer (for real) is nowhere. Mark was written first and his story has no birth narrative whatsoever. John is more of a theological work and his story has no birth narrative either. Matthew, whose background is 'high church' Jewish, writes from the perspective of Jesus' birth being the fulfillment of the Old Testament prophesy. In his story, the star appears to three kings or wise men, really astrologers . . . signifying royalty. But Luke, who was a Gentile and always befriended the downtrodden, the widows, the poor, the women, etc., has the angel appear to the lowly shepherds, in his version. All writers tell the story of God made flesh from their own perspective. I tell it in mine.

There is such a difference in fact and TRUTH. I believe that Christmas is about the simplicity of the TRUE message of love. Jesus was the channel through which the love of God was released into human history, simple enough to be born in a stable filled with hay and animals . . . not at all complicated. It is a message for kings—if they are willing to follow the light and shepherds alike—if they perceive the call of angels. All who are made aware can't remain where they are but must move toward the TRUTH—on their own journey through the deserts and plains and across hills and through valleys. Regardless of their journey they keep moving in the direction of the light and following.

The message of love is portrayed as simple as a twelve-year-old girl caring for her newborn, the best way she knows. The God-spirit bursting forth into the world with a message that speaks to the spirit of Christmas, a spirit of light—of hope overcoming fear and evil, even terrorism—hope overcoming darkness, grief, and the pain caused by the catastrophic event at Ground Zero—despair being overcome with hospitality and welcome—a message of compassion and an abiding love and peace, for which the whole world longs. At Christmas, Jesus births into our world the abundant inclusive love of God that crosses every human boundary.

Shelby Spong says it better than I can in his book Liberating the Gospels: "That is why Jesus was portrayed by Gospel writers as stepping across the racial divide to heal the Samaritan; or as stepping across the cultural divide to engage the woman at the well in conversation; or as stepping over the cultic purification laws to embrace the lepers; or as moving past that intensely human divide that enabled him to forgive his executioners. These are the kinds of things the love of God does, that love of God, which Christians believe they meet in Jesus, and has but one purpose—to invite us to be and to love us into being loving people . . ."

It really is such a simple message, a message simple enough to be born in a stable. I think that's why Jesus says that unless you become as little children . . . anyway, Jesus simply had the courage and freedom to be himself, in and under all sets of circumstances. Thus, he frees us to be ourselves; frees us from the need to impress others. This message calls us to love and be the self we are, the most real self, just as we are today. It is such a simple message, yet on many days, hard for me to accept.

Many people close to me have said things like, why did you tell "that" in your journal. In writing my journal I feel challenged to tell the truth, the real truth. However, in order to do that, I have really had to think about what the truth is, not just what might sound good, or make me sound good. What is my authentic, deepest self in these difficult situations? Hmmm.

At Christmas, love was ushered into the world in human form. Jesus was the jumper cable through which love surged into humanity, the conduit through which God flowed into the world, into every single person I have met at Ground Zero . . . or ever met, for that matter.

The message of Christmas is really very simple . . . you just open the door and your heart and say, "Come on in, I'll set another place for dinner. You are welcome here." You say it to only one person at a time, until you tell the whole world. A Merry Christmas indeed!

Printed in the United States
3665